بسم الله الرحمن الرحيم

THE SECRETS OF ASCETICISM

THE SECRETS OF ASCETICISM

BEING THE THIRD PART OF

Qam' al-Ḥirṣi Bi al-Zuhdi Wa al-Qanā'ah

IMAM AL-QURṬUBĪ

Introduced, Translated and Annotated by
ABŪ SĀLIF AḤMAD 'ALĪ AL-'ADANĪ

AMAL PRESS
BRISTOL • ENGLAND

Amal Press, PO Box 688, Bristol BS99 3ZR, England

http://www.amalpress.com
info@amalpress.com

 A CIP catalogue record for this book is available from the British Library

ISBN 978-0-9552359-6-2 paperback

Cover design Partners in Print | AAM

CONTENTS

My biggest debt of gratitude is owed to my companion Muḥsinah without whom this work would not have been possible, as she fueled my passion, believed in it, backed it up and egged me onto completing this translation.
I dedicate this book to the memories of my late father and my late shaykh Muḥammad ash-Shādhilī an-Nayfar.

TRANSLATOR'S INTRODUCTION

CONCERNING the approach to a classical text of a Muslim savant, one can think of two possible modes. One approach is to read it as a reminder, soul-enriching and consoling to some extent, of the greatness of our past, exemplified by living examples of the *dīn al-fiṭrah* and of the correct form and meaning of the Homo Islamicus. Thereafter the book is placed on a shelf, perhaps dusted off one more time or lent to a similar reader, and its value (nevertheless present) thereby exhausted.

As for the second approach, I am mindful of Heidegger's description of the fitting interaction with a work of art. As a work of art opens up vistas otherwise unknown, it must be entered into on its own terms for the discovery of Being to come to pass in that novel vista. Likewise we can enter into a work such as this, that opens up a vision of a manner of living, infused by Islam *ʿilman wa ʿamalan*, far removed from our present mortified condition. To read it thus is to walk inside that lush orchard, not with nostalgia or "dry" admiration, but so as to take on the human mould therein documented and absorb it into our being. By such reverential assimilation, the character of the exponents of such a practiced worldview penetrates into our consciousness and our daily acting out of the life transaction with Allāh.

As al-Qurṭubī himself indirectly states in the body of the translated text, the emulation of the leaders of the *dīn* is the very fundament of our way of life. Such emulation is a *dīn*, and it is a science, for one needs to know who he is taking from, and here, from the author down to the individuals he draws from, the reader is in safe hands.

It is thus hoped that the bulk of its readers will traverse the second such path of approaching a work like this, as a manual of instruction-cum-action.

II

One of the great benefits of many a classical text is the format used by those penning their kind. This format, pellucidly reflected in this work, is the pearlescent construction of the book through a variety of quotations from the Qur'ān, hadith literature, sayings of the great sages, anecdotes and stories, conceptual analyses embodied in concrete shapes, and the like thereof. Thus the reader is never overcome by ennui and he sees strewn before him an uninterrupted string of gems of guidance, from the divine to the human via the prophetic, across a river of multifarious generations.

In the ultimate analysis, in works such as this, the theme dealt with by the author is less important than what his dealing with it encompasses, or we could say, the pedagogical method of handling it. One could have exchanged for the subject of *zuhd* one of many other topics shedding light on the straight path, without having detracted from either the usefulness or the enjoyable nature of what is read. A thematic cornerstone of the *dīn*, such as *zuhd*, is like a ship sailing through the ocean of transformative Islamic knowledge. The voyaging through it, and the quality of the captain-scribe (al-Qurṭubī in our case), are more central tools than the conveyance instrument utilized.

While there is undoubted scope for the translation of more or less monothematic works of manifest worth to the present and future ummah, it is our modest opinion that more emphasis should be placed (and will be placed by us in our future endeavors, *inshallāh*) on these types of treasures of assorted wisdom. The accent will thus be put as much as possible on many-sided texts, embroidered with living examples of our predecessors—we acutely need to drink from what they have said or done, in zones of existence impinging on our daily lives.

III

Another inspirational key of this translation has been our desire to bring to the light of publication unearthed jewels of classical Islam, in particular from the region broadly known as the Islamic West (*al-gharb al-Islāmī*). There are a number of sound reasons for this preference of ours (shorn as it is of prejudicial exclusivity). One is the high qualitative level of such legacy. In this specific instance, the rank of al-Qurṭubī, not just as the writer of one of the best commentaries of the Qur'ān ever compiled, and the perfumed loftiness of the Andalusian heritage, are too obvious to the percipient reader to spend further elucidatory words thereon.

A second motive is that, to a large extent, the textual milestones of the Islamic West, of crucial significance in an age of formidable expansion of the Muslims' polity throughout the western countries, have been largely ignored by translators, whether into the English language or other vernaculars. So much so that the available classical literature in English tends to concentrate more and more on a few selected names of authors monopolizing the eyes of prospective buyers scanning the shelves of ordinary or cyber bookstores.

Thirdly, the Islamic West, of all geopolitical realities, has been traditionally the only one where the people have uncompromisingly held to a pure version of Islam, and by that I mean the *manhaj* of Ahl al-Sunnah wa al-Jamāᶜah, thereby increasing the reliability of their output for Muslims assailed by all kind of sectarian propaganda filling the stocks of published material.

IV

The full title of the Arabic text is *Qamᶜ al-ḥirṣi bi al-zuhdi wa al-qanāᶜah wa raddu dhull al-su'āli bi al-kutubi wa al-shafāᶜah*, i.e., *The curbing of covetousness by doing-without and contentment, and repelling the abasement of asking by books and intercession*. A variant which has been cited is *Qaṣr al-ḥirṣ*, with the meaning of the lowering or reduction of cupidity. The word *radd* could be variously rendered as resisting, opposing, warding off, rejecting, or driving back or away. The correct spelling might be *katbi*, which would signify writing instead of books. One should not be oblivious of the fact that copyists of manuscripts dispensed with diacritical points, let alone vowelling of words.

Strictly speaking it is an opus of *fiqh*, which goes on to prove the aforementioned point of richly-layered, three-dimensional, non-academic works treating subject matters in a miscellany of different facets.

The entire work, in fact, is devoted to a single question and the unifying thread it moves through: What is permissible in terms of asking other people and what is not, and the explanation of the virtue of patient reticence restraining one from asking. He spreads out this question in 40 chapters altogether, talking within the folds of such interlaced beads about contentment and its subdivisions, and about *zuhd* and its states.

The section on *zuhd* is the third one of the overall book. It consists of 13 chapters and it is in the form of a self-contained unit, which can (and has been) published in Arabic on its own. The corresponding chapter numbers of the greater Arabic text are in parentheses following the chapter number in this work.

Should the translation of this segment prove successful, it would be our desire to bring forth a new edition embracing the translation of the whole text, possibly by attaching thereto as an appendix excerpts from other renowned classical works on *zuhd* that have been published in the Arab world, of which more later.

V

As the Sufi of the *fuqahā'*, Aḥmad al-Zarrūq has affirmed, Sufism has been defined in countless ways, such that we could practically trace to every great Sufi a different definition thereof peculiar to him, because their tastes thereof differed. That is so, because it is a living dimension and they experientially traveled in it. That is why, in the *Ḥilyah*, Abū Nuʿaym "adorned" (the word *ḥilyah* meaning decorative adornment) each of the friends or members of the elite he gave a biographical account of with the definition of Sufism best personifying his tasting and expression of.

Likewise with the reality of *zuhd*, no definition can be exhaustive or even aims to be so. It has been defined, understood, interpreted, and enacted in many ways, depending on the visual angle it has been examined from.

All of the interpretive emphases quoted by the author are true, and each reader will naturally find his watering place among the semantic tributaries branching from its core linguistic signification.

The Madinans, for instance, from al-Zuhrī to the Mālikiyyah via Mālik b. Anas and Sufyān b. ʿUyaynah, in their terse clarity and illuminated avoidance of any tightening encumbrance in Islam, pertinently stressed the equation of *zuhd* with the discarding of dubious superfluities. Others, such as ʿAbdallāh b. al-Mubārak, likewise appropriately, placed the beat on the action of the heart turning away from this World, i.e., not to be owned by anything as opposed to not own anything. In this connection, one notices a number of significant aspects:

a) The common sense extolling of the value of wealth when used rightly. Ibn Rushd the grandfather considered it more meritorious than poverty or even mere sufficiency, unless frittered away in obnoxious pursuits. The Andalusian Muslims, in general, frowned upon begging and lauded man's efforts to earn a living;

b) The supreme instances of generosity of the sires mentioned by the author, with the companions in their vanguard, something to marvel at but even more so to restore in the present age. All of that was built on wealth-creation, and in this context one has to read the writer's staunch defense of ʿAbd al-Raḥmān b. ʿAwf ﷺ vis-à-vis the forged hadith, Shīʿī-inclined, which despised wealth, misleadingly made it synonymous with absence of *zuhd*, and lent credence to the sinister legend that only the likes of Abū Dharr al-Ghifārī ﷺ and the poor among the *muhājirūn*, had a valid title to an unbroken following of the Prophetic Sunnah. The mushrooming in the first eras of *al-bāqiyāt al-ṣāliḥāt*, to borrow a well-known Qur'ānic term, whether documented knowledge or *awqāf* or other species, was founded on wealth well-acquired and well-disposed of;

c) The median, balanced judgment of the true *fuqahā'*, exemplified by the *mīzān* of ʿAbdallāh b. Masʿūd on the issue of eating the food of the host whose wealth is partially tainted by usurious gains, or the one of the judge Abū Bakr b. al-ʿArabī (a typical feature of the Madinans) when censuring the identification of any form of asking with disobedience to the Creator.

Yet a third group, insightfully, linked *zuhd* to the lessening of one's worldly hope and from there to love of death, distinct as such from wishing death for oneself. Time has indeed proved that the Muslims' attachment to the "flower of the *dunyā*," life and wealth first and foremost, but especially the latter, is the great *fitnah* of this nation and the major stumbling block to its revival. Linguistically, *zuhd* is the opposite of *raghbah* or desire, which is a species of will. What predominates now is a desire to possess, escorted by the abasement of the Muslims. What prevailed yesteryear was a lack of volition to possess, accompanied by an abundance of means that the great Muslims did not escape from and which did not escape from them. Ibn Taymiyyah mentioned that lack of volition did not denote lack of love for the thing possessed, *zuhd* meaning the disappearance of volition and dislike for the thing in question at the same time. The use of means is separate from their elevation to a goal in themselves. Thus we encounter in Islam the expression: *al-zuhd fi al-zuhd*, to exercise *zuhd* about *zuhd*, to wit, that the *zāhid* should belittle what he exercises *zuhd* in.

Zuhd, in other words, is not a void. The absence of stimulation of desire, for dubious redundancies, for excessive hope, for perpetuity of worldly life, for one's self, implies the stimulation of desire for good. Thus the good flowed copiously and was circulated in a vortex for everyone's benefit. *Zuhd* and generosity, as the anecdotal accounts of al-Qurtubī establish beyond doubt, are inseparable twins. Yaḥyā b. Muʿādh relevantly said: "The distinguishing sign of *zuhd* is to be generous with the existent." And it was said to one of the great men: "What did *zuhd* lead them to?" He replied: "To solacing friendliness with Allāh, not to a void of renunciation pure and simple."

One should also remark the exacting delineation of the scope of *zuhd*, that is, the six areas where it operates. It is patently clear from such crucial demarcating exercise that marriage, for instance, falls outside its scope, as the story of the self-misleading "worshippers" who visited the apartments of the wives of the Prophet ﷺ illustrates. The locus of *zuhd* is not left to the self's whims and self-orientation. It is defined by Allāh and His Rasūl ﷺ and as such accords with shariah parameters. As one of the erudite predecessors has said: They were only deprived arrival (*al-wuṣūl*) by laying the roots (*al-'uṣūl*) to waste. If the roots of *zuhd* specify its praiseworthiness in matters of attire but not in matters of marital expansion, for example, tampering with such roots by their deracinating inversion and so forth, will preclude the would-be *zāhid's* reaching the fruits of the tree of *zuhd*.

The rest can be worked out analogically. Means of transport, for instance, are not included in the catalogue of the *mazhūd fīhi*, i.e., the thing one exercises *zuhd* in, since the abundant breeding of animals was recommended for the purpose of equipping the Islamic military forces and strengthening the caliphate. Yet vying with one another in expensive cars has more to do, nowadays, with the image consciousness and luxury spending on attire than with fulfilling the erstwhile purpose of transportation. Again, one looks at the roots without being deceived by the ostensible branches.

Let us string some pearls of indicia together: The luxuriant clothing, the nice processed food, vehicles as image-projecting status symbols, the house to be ignored "because the man busy around it built it only so that it be looked at," as the dismissive al-Thawrī mentions in one of the anecdotal accounts in this book. Then the *zāhid* Muslim moving in the opposite direction would have been saved from the incarceration of the whole consumerist cycle.

The fine balancing act is expressed in the most eloquent way in the following verse:

Seek the abode of the akhira *with what Allāh has given you, without forgetting your portion of the* dunyā (28:77).

VI

The centrality of *zuhd* can be gauged not only by the fact that sections consecrated thereto are found in all the major collections of hadith (be they the *Ṣaḥīḥayn*, the works of *Sunan*, Aḥmad's *Musnad* or the *Muṣannafāt* such as those of ʿAbd al-Razzāq or Ibn Abī Shaybah), but also by the far-reaching literature dedicated specifically to this topic.

1) The most essential works in this category are the following: the imam and *ḥāfiẓ*, Shaykh al-Islām ʿAbdallāh b. al-Mubārak (d. 181 AH) wrote *al-Zuhd wa al-raqā'iq*, which has been published in Arabic;

2) The imam al-Muʿāfā b. ʿImrān al-Mawṣilī (d. 185 AH). The *ḥāfiẓ* al-Dhahabī mentioned in *Tadhkirat al-ḥuffāẓ* that al-Muʿāfā authored works on Prophetic *sunan* and one on *zuhd, inter alia;*

3) The *muḥaddith* and *ḥāfiẓ* Muḥammad b. Fuḍayl b. Ghazwān al-Kūfī (d. 195 AH). The *ḥāfiẓ* al-Dhahabī said in *Tadhkirat al-ḥuffāẓ* that he penned *al-Zuhd, al-Duʿā'* and other works;

4) The imam and *muḥaddith* Wakī' b. al-Jarrāḥ (d. 197 AH), one of Aḥmad b. Ḥanbal's *shuyūkh*, wrote a treatise on *zuhd* which was published in the 1980s for the first time;

5) The imam and *faqīh* Aḥmad b. Ḥanbal (d. 241 AH) likewise composed a celebrated work on this subject, published in Arabic in various editions;

6) The *ḥāfiẓ* and *zāhid* Hannād b. al-Sarī (d. 243 AH), a disciple of the aforesaid Wakī' b. al-Jarrāḥ and the Shaykh of al-Kūfah in his age, whose book on *zuhd*

has similarly emerged in published form in the 1980s;

7) Imam Abū Bakr ᶜAbdallāh b. Muḥammad, known as Ibn Abi al-Dunyā (d. 281 AH). His work on *zuhd* exists in manuscript form in the library of Aḥmad al-Thālith, in 126 pages, under reference number 591;

8) The *ḥāfiẓ* and *ᶜālim* Ibrāhīm b. al-Junayd (d. ca. 260 AH), to whom al-Khaṭīb al-Baghdādī attributed books on the subjects of *zuhd* and heart-softening matters (*al-raqā'iq*), as reported by the *ḥāfiẓ* al-Dhahabī in *Tadhkirat al-ḥuffāẓ*;

9) The *ᶜallāmah* and qadi Abū Aḥmad Muḥammad b. Aḥmad al-ᶜAssāl al-Aṣbahānī (d. 249 AH), among whose works the *ḥāfiẓ* al-Dhahabī enumerates *Kitāb al-raqā'iq* in *Tadhkirat al-ḥuffāẓ*;

10) Aḥmad b. ᶜAmr b. Abī ᶜĀṣim al-Shaybānī (d. 287 AH). His *Kitāb al-zuhd*, on Sufism and *zuhd*, was published by Dār al-Kutub al-ᶜIlmiyyah in Beirut in 1988;

11) The *ḥāfiẓ* Abū Ḥafṣ ᶜUmar b. Aḥmad, known as Ibn Shāhīn (d. 385 AH). The *ḥāfiẓ* al-Dhahabī said about him in *Tadhkirat al-ḥuffāẓ*: He compiled *Kitāb al-zuhd*, divided in 100 sections.

There are of course other such notable works.

Al-Qurṭubī, who postdates all the abovementioned luminaries, was aware of such rich heritage, whence his prefatory words (at the commencement of the entire work, meaning the first third thereof): "I aimed at gathering a book expanding on the meaning of the works of my predecessors thereto, and building further on the foundations contained therein."

He has indeed achieved his stated objective, which attainment adds further justification to our decision to translate his "improving completion on his antecedents' building blocks."

But over and above the centrality signaled by such literary output, the essentiality of *zuhd* for the Muslims is perfectly captured by the author's quotation of Ibn Masᶜūd's qualitative comparison between the generation of the companions and the following, more seemingly "pious" generation, and his connection thereof to the increasing curve of Muslims' attachment to this World.

VII

In our translation, we have sought to strike an equilibrium between faithfulness to the text, the preservation of the flavor of classical Arabic and the characteristic expressive style associated with it, and an intelligible rendering thereof in fluent modern English.

We further deemed it fit to include as many biographical references as possible, since knowledge of the bygone masters we take from is itself most desired for our *dīn* in our present epoch.

We aimed at clarifying possible ambiguities in the text, indicating those passages where the Arabic manuscript presents lacunae, and referring the reader to further sources for self-illumination.

It was not our intention to run commentaries on the Qur'ānic verses or Prophetic *aḥādīth* quoted in the text, for that would have rendered this agile manual cumbersome and run counter to the inspiring idea behind the author's treatment of his subject. We nevertheless endeavored to trace all textual authorities to their original loci, so that the committed reader could further his engrossment with the topic by visiting such mapped out sites and their commentaries.

If this translator's time and energies have met with some reward, and Allāh is the grantor of *thawāb*, it is purely by His Generous Bounty.

Any error or imprecision is to be ascribed to my human defectiveness. Readers are kindly encouraged to point them out and put forward any constructive suggestions for improvement on this, *wa mā tawfīqiya illā billāh.*

Abū Sālif Aḥmad ʿAlī al-ʿAdanī
Johannesburg, 30 September 2006

BIOGRAPHY OF IMAM AL-QURṬUBĪ

He is Muḥammad b. Aḥmad b. Abū Bakr b. Farḥ al-Anṣārī al-Khazrajī al-Andalusī, Abū ʿAbdallāh al-Qurṭubī. Abū ʿAbdallāh was his *kunyā* or patronymic name. Al-Anṣārī is a noun of ascription showing that his lineage was traceable back to the Madinan Anṣār, and al-Khazrajī that it specifically connected him genealogically to the Khazraj, one of the two main tribes of al-Madīnah together with the Aws, though to be more precise the reference is to the Khazārijah who settled in al-Andalus.

The Andalusian and the one from Cordova, his city in Islamic Spain, are self-evidently intelligible nouns of further ascription.

BIRTH, FAMILY, AND EARLY GROWTH

Oddly, though we know the precise day of his departure from this World, all his biographers have failed to attribute him to even a specific year for his birth, let alone a particular day or day of the week.

That, together with the general paucity of biographical details about his person, over the centuries, has caused modern scholars to ask questions about his family milieu, especially whether he came from a home of fame and material blessing or one of poverty and obscure indigence, and whether he grew up safely by his parents' side or as an orphan tutored and monitored by some relative of his.

The key to unravelling the riddle is not found externally in some biographical gloss, but inside the author's own opus. When commenting, in fact on Sūrah

Āl ᶜImrān (169–170), where Allāh describes the state of the *shuhadā'*, alive and provided by their Lord to their satisfaction, he mentioned in his *tafsīr*, in his treatment of the fifth *mas'alah* derived from such pair of Qur'ānic signs, that the enemy attacked Cordova in the early hours of the morning, when the victims were neglectful of their ambushing presence near their stone basins, and killed some of them, his own father included, while taking others captive. The author wanted to know whether his father's rank was that of a *shahīd* killed in battle or whether the ruling pertaining to him was that of the rest of the deceased believers. He sought clarification from his shaykh and teacher Abū Jaᶜfar Aḥmad, who advised him to perform the ritual bath on him and pray over him because he had not been killed among the rows of fighters in the battlefield. His other shaykh Rabīᶜ b. ᶜAbd al-Raḥmān b. Aḥmad b. Rabīᶜ supplied him with the opposite answer to the very same question. He then proceeded to pose it for the third time to *qāḍī al-jamāᶜah* (a high judicial post), Abū al-Ḥasan ᶜAlī, while he was surrounded by a group of jurisprudents, and he reverted him to the first view (only adding thereto that he should place him in a shroud before praying over his corpse). Al-Qurṭubī acted by his judgment. Thereafter, when his knowledge was more advanced, he came across the verification of the correct position in this *mas'alah* in Abū al-Ḥasan al-Lakhmī's *al-Tabṣirah* and other extolled works, so he commented: Had I known it beforehand, I would not have performed the *ghusl* on his dead body, but I would have buried him with all the bloodstains on the clothes he was wearing at the time of his death.

He was thus raised by his father, in whose custody he remained until the latter's death as a *shahīd* according to the correct juristic view. His father worked in the field of agriculture, and was directly overseeing the harvesting of one species of farming produce when he met his death at the hands of the assailing Christians in Cordova, in the year 627 AH, during the early morning of the third day of Ramaḍān.

Cordova was at that stage under the leadership of Muḥammad b. Yūsuf b. Hūd (d. 635 AH), who had succeeded in removing the yoke of the Muwaḥḥidūn and summoned obedience to himself which spread in a number of Andalusian fortresses including Murcia and Badajoz. For that reason, the Christians spotted a danger in his rule and carried out a number of ruthless raids against his possessions, razing villages and spoiling cultivated tills in the process. The assault which resulted in the death of the author's father might have been engineered by the troops of Ferdinand III, the then King of Castilla, after the preparatory work carried out by his father Alfonso IX.

Ambiguity still permeates the date of birth of al-Qurṭubī, but from the said biographical reference in his *tafsīr* one might safely assume that he was born during the rule of the Muwaḥḥidūn, probably in the course of the caliphate of Yaᶜqūb b. Yūsuf b. ᶜAbd al-Mu'min, between 580 and 595 AH, and Allāh knows best.

HIS LEARNING

At a young age enabling him to receive the first rudiments of knowledge, he studied Arabic and poetry side-by-side with learning the Qur'ān. That was in conformity with the pedagogical model followed by the Andalusians in contrast with the Muslim educationists of all the other Islamic regions. The great judge of Sevilla Abū Bakr b. al-ᶜArabī criticized it, since in his view the youth should be taught only language and poetry at first before moving to the study of the Qur'ān, which would become easier once approached from such solid initial foundation. Ibn Khaldūn at first praised Abū Bakr b. al-ᶜArabī's approach, but then he retraced his steps and clarified that, if a youngster accosted the learning of the Qur'ān at a somewhat advanced age, a barrier might interpose itself between him and reception of knowledge of the Book, or else worldly pursuits might engross him away from studies, and in that manner learning the Qur'ān would have eluded him.[1]

His furtherance of learning, with the ferocious resolution and unflinching perseverance so characteristic of the Andalusians, took him from one reputable circle of knowledge in Cordova to another, up to the point when he left his city having already accumulated a wealth of ᶜ*ilm* within his cognitive compass. Study circles were widespread in al-Andalus during his age, and Islamic learning rotated around mosques in conformity with the classical custom modern nation-states have wreaked havoc against.

TEACHERS IN AL-ANDALUS

In Cordova, one can again cite the ones he asked a *fatwa* from on the issue of his father's burial:

1) Aḥmad b. Muḥammad b. al-Qays, Abū Jaᶜfar, known as Ibn Abī Ḥijjah, eulogized by the historian Ibn al-Abbār as an *ᶜālim* in Arabic and Qur'ānic sciences. He wrote a number of works, including an abridgment of the *Ṣaḥīḥayn*. When Cordova fell into Christian hands in the year 633 AH, he moved first to Sevilla and then to Mallorca. The Christians however took him prisoner and subjected him to painful physical punishment, and he passed away shortly thereafter in Mallorca, in the year 643 AH. Many were the teachers he graduated under, including Abū al-Qāsim Khalaf b. Bashkuwāl (d. 578 AH), the prolific author of many books in manifold fields, and the Cordovan Ibn Maḍā' Aḥmad b. ᶜAbd al-Raḥmān (d. 592 AH), especially proficient in the Qur'ānic readings and the Prophetic hadith, beside his erudition in *fiqh*, *uṣūl*, *kalām*, and Arabic. Ibn Farḥūn described him as a person of generous temperament, courteous interaction, pure yearning, self-restraint in speech, truthfulness of word, full manhood, and excellent sharing of knowledge in disparate sciences with peers and their likes;

2) Rabīᶜ b. ᶜAbd al-Raḥmān b. Aḥmad b. ᶜAbd al-Raḥmān b. Rabīᶜ al-Ashᶜarī, Abū Sulaymān, also from the inhabitants of Cordova and their judge. A righteous and fair man in his judgments, of eminent social rank heading from a noble family, was how Ibn al-Abbār synthetically traced the contours of his virtue. His specialization was in hadith. He also left his hometown following its conquest by the Christians on Sunday, 23 Shawwāl of 633 AH, setting out for Sevilla where he met his death very shortly after his departure for it. One of his own *shuyūkh* was Abū Muḥammad Ḥawṭullāh (ᶜAbdallāh b. Sulaymān b. Dāwud b. ᶜUmar al-Anṣārī, d. 612 AH in Granada), originally from Valencia, a master of many disciplines who acted by his knowledge and sternly avoided the people of innovation and whims. His corpse was transferred to Malaga where he is buried;

3) His full brother Yaḥyā b. ᶜAbd al-Raḥmān b. Aḥmad b. ᶜAbd al-Raḥmān b. Rabīᶜ al-Ashᶜarī al-Qurṭubī (b. 553 AH), a judge in Cordova before its fall and later in Granada, who died in Malaga after being affected by hemiplegia in the year 639 or 640 AH He was extremely humble, a precise researcher, a gentle dia-

lectician and a staunch defender of the Sunnah. He is probably the one referred to by the author when commenting that Abū al-Daḥdāḥ gave out in *ṣadaqah* his whole orchard comprising of 600 palm trees when he first heard the following verse: *Is there anyone who will make Allāh a generous loan so that He can multiply it for him many times over? Allāh both restricts and expands. And you will be returned to Him.* [Sūrah al-Baqarah, 2:243 in the *Warsh riwāyah*, 2:245 in others.]

TRIP TO EGYPT

His knowledge was already firmly rooted and branching out in multifarious directions when he travelled to Egypt. His age at that stage has been left unspecified in his biographies. We know from his *tafsīr* that the enemy once passed by him seated in an open space two times without noticing his presence, protected by Allāh with a *ḥijāb mastūr*, "an obscuring veil," as He similarly concealed the Prophet ﷺ from the approaching wife of Abū Lahab, al-ʿAwrā' Umm Jamīl bint Ḥarb, while sitting with Abū Bakr in the mosque. [See Sūrah al-Isrā', 17:45.] After that recorded experience of miraculous divine assistance, he safely returned to Cordova, which he left with the bulk of its grieving inhabitants during the month of Shawwāl of 633 AH We ignore whether he directed himself at once to Egypt or whether he spent a period in another fortified city of Islamic Spain such as Valencia or Sevilla, until it, too, was conquered by the enemy (the latter in 642 AH). What we are told by the surviving accounts is that he first resided in Alexandria, a typical stopover for the exiled Andalusians migrating by land or by sea, prior to 648 AH (the year of Ibn al-Rawwāj's death), before settling down definitively in Upper Egypt.

In Alexandria he studied under the imam and *muḥaddith* Abū Muḥammad ʿAbd al-Wahhāb b. Rawwāj (b. 554 AH). He also got in contact with the *shuyūkh* attached to the schools of Abū Bakr al-Ṭurṭūshi (from Tortosa in al-Andalus), Ibn ʿAwf and the *ḥāfiẓ* al-Salafī.

Al-Ṭurṭūshi, who wrote core works, some of which have been published, such as his political treatise *Sīrāj al-mulūk* and *al-Ḥawādith wa al-bida'*, was one of the topmost Mālikī *fuqahā'* in his age, an acting-ʿ*ālim* and scrupulous *zāhid* of marked humility and contentment with little. He arrived in Alexandria when the city was in the grip of fear and the Islamic landmarks fundamentally paralyzed, given that the majority of the sages, belonging to the Madinan *madhhab*, were under the oppression of the official methodology of the ruling Fatimids. The fearless al-Ṭurṭūshi, however, openly started to teach and spread the knowledge of the Madinans despite the tight grip of Shīʿī domination. One of his students was the other *zāhid* al-Ṭāhir b. ʿAwf (d. 581 AH), the first teacher of the earliest *madrasah* in Alexandria, titled after him al-Madrasat al-ʿAwfiyyah, where Islamic sciences were studied. Another student of his was the *ḥāfiẓ* al-Salafī, Abū al-Ṭāhir Aḥmad b. Muḥammad al-Aṣbahānī al-Shāfiʿī (d. 576 AH), originally from Isfahan, and resident in Alexandria since 511 AH He was one of the imams of hadith, *fiqh*, and Arabic.

It is in this milieu, revived by the breeze of life al-Ṭurṭūshi and his disciples injected into the stagnancy al-Ṭurṭūshi had found upon his arrival, that most of al-Qurṭubī's Alexandrine *shuyūkh* emerged and developed. Apart from the aforementioned imam in hadith and *fiqh*, Ibn al-Rawwāj (whose name was Ẓāfir b. ʿAlī b. Fattūḥ al-Azdī al-Iskandarānī al-Mālikī), the shaykh, imam, and *muḥaddith* rightly-guided in the *dīn*, and the *musnid* of Alexandria, as al-Dhahabī praised him, who had come out of al-Salafī's school and received oral transmission of knowledge from Ibn ʿAwf, we encounter:

1) The *ʿallāmah* Ibn al-Jumayzī, Bahā' al-Dīn Abū al-Ḥasan ʿAlī b. Hibatillāh al-Lakhmī al-Miṣrī al-Shāfiʿī, a much-traveled *ʿālim* who heard al-Bukhārī's *Sahīh* from Ibn ʿAsākir in Damascus, *inter alia.* He also studied under al-Salafī and Ibn ʿAwf. Al-Dhahabī lauded his status of shaykh in hadith. He was the *khaṭīb* of the Jāmiʿ mosque in Cairo, as related by al-Subkī, and the head of the *ʿulamā'* in that city, where he taught and issued fatwas for a period. He was very majestic. His own teacher Ibn Abī ʿAṣrūn placed over his head and shoulders the shawl-like garment known as the *ṭaylasān* as an ennobling mark distinguishing him from his fellow students and contemporaries. He knew *tafsīr* as well, and undoubtedly our author studied that science, where he was created to excel, with him, as well as, quite likely, the Shāfiʿī *fiqh*. Al-Qurṭubī was a sober follower of Mālik, who had no qualms in disagreeing with his imam, as in the *mas'alah* of the ablution-performer's involuntary swallowing of a little water while rinsing one's mouth during fasting, if the stronger shariah proof so demanded;

2) One of the leading imams, not a direct student of al-Salafī and Ibn ʿAwf, though he breathed the cultural air of their school, Abū al-ʿAbbās Aḥmad b. ʿUmar b. Ibrāhīm al-Mālikī al-Qurṭubī (578–656 AH), born and bred in Cordova,

where he already achieved proficiency in Islamic sciences before emigrating to Alexandria. There, too, he attained widespread fame (embracing both the East and the West), first and foremost in *fiqh* and Arabic. His most famous work is his commentary on Muslim's *Ṣaḥīḥ*, *al-Mufhim fī sharḥi Ṣaḥīḥi Muslim*, which is like the dough on which al-Māzirī, al-Qāḍī ʿIyāḍ, al-Nawawī (most extensively of them all) and al-Ubbī leavened their subsequent commentaries thereon building reliantly on it. Our author heard from him parts of the said work;

3) Al-Ḥasan b. Muḥammad al-Bakrī (574–656 AH), al-Taymī al-Naysābūrī then al-Dimashqī, Abū ʿAlī Ṣadr al-Dīn, another extensive traveller (nicknamed al-Raḥḥāl by the historians), born in Damascus, and an imam, *muḥaddith*, and historian of fine features and an eloquent tongue, though, for a period, he was not shorn of weaknesses such as excessive and exaggerated claims, passing over the explanation of difficult words, mixing things up, and a penchant for impudent jocularity and a prankster's jesting. He also remained semi-paralyzed in the latter part of his life. In any event, our author studied under him when both his character and his knowledge were integral and free from such transient deterioration, probably in Alexandria, as was also the more likely case in respect of Ibn al-Rawwāj. At the same time, his reception of knowledge from Ibn al-Jumayzī and al-Bakrī (who rested from his many travels and resided at the end of his days therein) took place in Cairo according to the more preponderant view, during the time span preceding the author's settlement in Upper Egypt.

In addition to all the people already mentioned above, the author transmitted hadith from Abū al-Ḥasan ʿAlī b. Muḥammad b. ʿAlī b. Ḥafṣ al-Yaḥṣubī.

DEATH

Al-Qurṭubī finally put roots in the city of Upper Egypt, north of Asyūṭ and east of the Nile, then called Munyah Banī Khaṣīb (taking its name from an individual, al- Khaṣīb or Ibn al-Khaṣīb), where he died in the night of Monday, 9 Shawwāl 671 AH, the equivalent of 29 April 1273 AD, and where he is buried [It is the present-day al-Munyā]. No indication of the reason for his final residential choice has been handed down to us by either his biographers or by himself. His grave is visited to draw blessings from. In 1971, a large mosque named after him was built in an area known as "Arḍ Sulṭān" bi al-Munyā. It includes a mausoleum where his remnants have been transferred from his erstwhile grave.

HIS CHARACTER

All his biographers concur with al-Dāwudī's summation of his character, after mentioning that the travelling ʿ*ulamā* moved around with his *tafsīr* within their reach: "He was one of the righteous slaves of Allāh, knowledgeable savants, and practitioners of *zuhd* in this World, engrossed by the matters of the Afterlife, his time enlivened by effort,[2] ʿ*ibādah*, and writing (...). He discarded affectation and walked in a single garment, a white cotton skullcap on his head."

The *zuhd* of al-Qurṭubī did not consist in self-deprivation of good things, but in not making the pursuit of nice provisions and pleasures a goal of his life, his ultimate focus in the Hereafter impeding the sovereignty of this World over his existential domain. In his *tafsīr*, he attacked the distorted understanding of *zuhd* held by some Muslims, and asserted that the beautification of oneself by wearing nice clothes when meeting people in no way negated the practice of *zuhd*, the choice of patched garments being that of the persons affecting *zuhd*. In *Nafḥ al-ṭīb*, indeed, the Andalusian al-Maqqarī, from his exile in Greater Syria, stressed that the Andalusians, of all nations, were the most concerned with the cleanliness of their clothing, so much so that one of them might be without daily food and retreat at night fasting and with an empty stomach, but he would not fail nonetheless to buy soap to wash his dress and make it look sparkling clean when moving around outdoors. The author's lack of affectation must thus be viewed in this context excluding any filthy appearance or shabby dressing. As Ayyūb al-Sakhtiyānī stated, *zuhd* in what Allāh has decreed to be *ḥalāl* is but the third, last, and lowliest form of *zuhd*.

Al-Qurṭubī, a devout worshipper, was extremely scrupulous in matters of the *dīn*, but that did not prevent him from advocating the permissibility of the monetary grants of monarchs and emirs, as laid out fully in the thirteenth and conclusive chapter of this work.

Here we have a typical paradigm of the middle-of-the-road, well-poised savant from the Islamic West.

HIS ʿAQĪDA

As it is amply demonstrated by his *tafsīr*, al-Qurṭubī, echoing in that the majority of the ʿ*ulamā'* of al-Andalus, was a follower of the ʿ*aqīdah* of Ahl al-Sunnah in its Ashʿarite form, which he defended against the attacks especially of the Muʿtazilah, given the popularity of the Muʿtazilite creed among numerous Andalusian scholars.

HIS INTELLECTUAL LEGACY

A versatile, alert, and sagacious *ʿallāmah* and reliable *ḥāfiẓ* who had plunged himself in the sea of knowledge, as reflected in his books evincing abundant reading, deep understanding and erudition, his imamate and his far-reaching merit, was how al-Dhahabī described him, though his terse acknowledgment of his virtue and achievements does not render full justice to them. A knowledgeable imam who dived into the meanings of *aḥādīth*, wrote elegantly and had the gift of correct transmission, was Ibn al-ʿImād's description of our man.

Al-Qurṭubī had many students, but they are covered in obscurity. He gave an *ijāzah* to his own son Shihāb al-Dīn Abū al-ʿAbbās Aḥmad. He might be Ibn Farḥ al-Ishbīlī, due to the undermentioned, having grown up in that city since the age of eight after the fall of Cordova. Ibn Farḥ al-Ishbīlī fell captive to the Christians besieging Sevilla, and was later rescued from their hands by Allāh. He was thus empowered to relocate to Egypt where he studied with the prominent *shuyūkh* of the age, before he took up residence in Damascus, studying in the Umawī Mosque therein and excelling in the Prophetic hadith. The shaykhdom of hadith studies at Dār al-Ḥadīth al-Nūriyyah was offered to him, but he declined the post. He passed away on 9 Jumāda al-Ākhirah, 699 AH.

Fortunately for us, more is known, and in a number of cases firsthand, about the works he authored, themselves attesting on their own to the conceded breadth of his learning:

1) His noble *tafsīr*, one of the greatest, most comprehensive, renowned, consulted, valued and valuable ever, *al-Jāmiʿ li-aḥkām al-Qur'ān wa al-mubayyin li mā taḍḍamanahū min al-Sunnah wa āyi al-furqān*, known simply as the *Tafsīr of al-Qurṭubī*, published in countless editions, scholarly and otherwise. A treasure trove not just for the interpretation of verses of legal judgments, for which it is justly celebrated, but for all aspects of Qur'ānic knowledge and sciences. Probably commenced in al-Andalus, albeit not in Cordova, it was completed during his stay in Upper Egypt;

2) An encyclopaedic compendium on the otherworldly states of the *barzakh* and the Hereafter, presently the most known such work in the field, whether

classical or modern, loved and respected by all, *al-Tadhkirah fī aḥwāl al-mawtā wa umūri al-ākhirah*, likewise published in many glossy and well-annotated editions;

3) *Al-Tadhkār fī afḍal al-adhkār*, a lovely work on Allāh's Book, similar in style to al-Nawawī's *al-Tibyān* but more complete and filled with knowledge than it (as remarked by al-Dāwūdī), dealing with a wide array of issues such as the etiquette of handling the Book, matters of ʿ*aqīdah* related to it, dimensions of Qur'ānic sciences, and virtues of the Qur'ān and of single *suwar* thereof. It has been published in Arabic, and is eminently suitable for a translation into English;

4) *Al-Iʿlām bi mā fī dīn al-naṣārā min al-mafāsidi wa al-awhām, wa iẓhāru maḥāsini dīn al-Islām*, a precious book, similarly published in Arabic, where he refutes the delusions and exposes the corruption of the Christian religion, and underpins by comparison the virtuous merits of Islam;

5) *Qamʿ al-ḥirṣi bi al-zuhdi wa al-qanāʿah wa raddu dhull al-su'āli bi al-kutubi wa al-shafāʿah*, which is the book this translation is devoted to as far as its third section is concerned. The full text, too, has appeared in Arabic. Ibn Farḥūn mentioned that he had read no better book on the topic than the subject matter of our translation, and that is something, given the said lofty company of authors and authored works preceding him in this balsamic field;

6) *Faḍā'il al-Qur'ān wa ādāb al-tilāwah*, a work ascribed to the author and published in Egypt by al-Maktab al-Thaqāfī, edited by Aḥmad Ḥijāzī al-Saqā, which overlaps in many chapters with number 3 hereabove, and fundamentally deals, in a shorter form, with the same range of subject matters;

7) *Al-Asnā fī sharḥi asmā' Allāh al-ḥusnā*, one of the finest classical works on the beautiful divine names;

8) *Al-Taqrīb li kitāb al-tamhīd*, also referred to by most of his biographers as *Sharḥ al-taqaṣṣī*, a gloss on Ibn ʿAbd al-Barr's famous commentary of *al-Muwaṭṭa'* endeavoring to ease the comprehension thereof. It is in two huge volumes, in manuscript form, in the library of the Qarawiyyīn Mosque in Fez;

9) *Risālah fī al-qābi al-ḥadīth*. In manuscript form (in Algiers);

10) *Al-Miṣbāḥ fī al-jamʿi bayn al-afʿāli wa al-ṣaḥḥāḥ*, a linguistic work gathering al-Jawharī's *al-ṣaḥḥāḥ* and Ibn al-Qaṭṭā' s *al-Afʿāl*, in manuscript form (in Berlin);

11) *Al-Muqtabas fī sharḥi Muwaṭṭa' Mālikī b. Anas*;

12) *Manhaj al-ʿibādah wa maḥajjat al-sālikīna wa al-zuhhād*, ostensibly a work related thematically to the present one;

13) *Al-Lumaʿ al-lu'lu'iyyah fī sharḥi al-ʿishrīnāt al-nabawiyyah*, on hadith as number 9;

14) *Al-Intihāz fī qirā'ati Ahl al-Kūfah wa al-Baṣrah wa al-Shām wa Ahl al-Ḥijāz*, on the different modes of Qur'ānic recitation;

15) A poem (*Urjūzah*) where he gathered all the names of the Prophet ﷺ.

THE SECRETS OF ASCETICISM

BEING THE THIRD PART OF

Qamᶜ al-Ḥirṣi Bi al-Zuhdi Wa al-Qanāᶜah

IMAM AL-QURṬUBĪ

CHAPTER 1 (28)

ZUHD AND ITS EXPLANATION

Allāh has said *We made everything on the earth adornment for it so that we could test them to see whose actions are the best* (Qur'ān, 18:7). Sufyān al-Thawrī ﷺ has stated, in relation to the words "whose actions are the best," that they mean: [To see] who exercises the greatest *zuhd* in relation to it, i.e., the adornment.[3] Likewise, Abū ʿAṣṣām al-ʿAsqalānī commented about the same phrase: Those who forgo it the most.[4] The word *zuhd*, in the speech of the Arabs, signifies the following: *Turning away from wealth and fame.*

Al-Jawharī and other linguists have asserted that *zuhd* is the opposite of desire. One says in Arabic: *Zahida fi al-shay'* or *ʿan al-shay', yazhadu zuhdan wa zahādatan.*[5] *Zahada yazha du* is another morphological variant.[6] As for so-and-so *tazahhada*, it means *taʿabbada*, i.e., withdraw into devotional worship. *Al-tazahhhud fi al-shay'* or *ʿan al-shay'*[7] is the contrary of the stimulation of desire. And the word *al-muzhid*[8] means a man of scarce wealth.

In the prophetic hadith it has been reported that: "The best of people is the believer of little wealth (*mu'min muzhid*)."[9]

The connotation of the word *al-zahīd* is (the) "little". One says in Arabic: *Fulān zahīd al-akl*, i.e., "So-and-so eats little"; and *Wādin zahīd* means, "A valley that takes in little water." It is also said by the Arabs: *Khudh zuhda mā yakfīk*, that is, "Take the measured amount that suffices you"; as well as, *Fulān yazhadu ʿaṭā'a fulān*, "So-and-so esteems the gift of so-and-so as being little."[10]

The Prophet ﷺ was of all people the one with the highest level of *zuhd*, and the one who was the most self-sufficient, i.e., in want of the least amount of external material things. It suffices, on the issue of his *zuhd*, to relate what has been reported by al-Tirmidhī, Ibn Mājah, and others, on the authority of Abū Umāmah,[11] that he ﷺ said: "My Lord offered me the land of Makkah in its gold and silver equivalent. I said: 'No, Lord, rather I satiate myself with food one day and stay hungry another day, so that, when I am hungry I turn to You beseechingly and remember You, and when I eat to my full satisfaction I praise and thank You.'"[12] Al-Tirmidhī said it was a good (*ḥasan*)[13] hadith.

Zuhd was the state of Abū Bakr, ʿUmar, ʿAlī, Abū Dharr [al-Ghifārī], ʿUthmān, Abū al-Dardā', Tamīm al-Dārī and their likes. How many indeed were those who practised *zuhd* among the companions! ʿAbd al-Rahmān b. ʿAwf and al-Zubayr were both people of *zuhd*, and no heed is paid to the transmission of the one who narrated that ʿAbd al-Rahmān b. ʿAwf would enter *jannah* crawling, no one having previously narrated it. As for al-Zubayr, he had no equal. Allāh willing, examples of the states of those who practised *zuhd* in this world, and the modalities of their *zuhd*, will be mentioned hereafter.[14]

VARIANT ALLUSIONS TO *ZUHD* AMONG THE SAGES

Mālik b. Anas said that *zuhd* was *taqwā*. Our scholars[15] stated that he intended guarding oneself from dubious things, since man has ample room to maneuver in neutrally permissible things.[16]

Al-Musayyib b. Wāḍiḥ[17] asserted that Ibn ʿUyaynah was asked about *zuhd*, whereupon he replied: "To do without what Allāh has proscribed. As for what He has declared lawful, He has permitted it. Thus, the prophets ate, drank, and married."

Al-Zuhrī said that *zuhd* was not attained by ascetically mortifying the flesh, but rather by exercising self-restraint [and staying] away from the dubious things. It was further reported from him that he was questioned as to what *zuhd* in this life was, and he responded as follows: "Not to let the forbidden overcome your patient self-restraint, or the permitted your thankfulness."

Sufyān al-Thawrī and those who took from him said: "Reducing and curbing hope. It does not lie in eating coarse food or wearing a woollen wrap." That is a fine statement, since the one whose hope is lessened and held back turns away from this World and devotes his full energy to worshipping the Master.[18]

Ibn Zurārah b. Awfā,[19] after the death of Sufyān al-Thawrī, said to him: "May

Allāh show mercy on you. What were you told?" He turned away from me [Ibn Zurārah b. Awfā], and then I said:[20] "What did Allāh do with you?" He was receptive to me on hearing the question put to him that way, and he answered: "Allāh has bestowed favor on me by His generosity and kindness." I asked him: "Which action in your knowledge best helps one attain the goal?" "Content-ment,"[21] he replied, and a limited hope.

Some people, on the other hand, maintained that *zuhd* meant to loathe en-comium and the love of praise.[22]

I said: This is an allusive reference by him to the fact that to forgo the whole of this World is the most loved form of forgoing it.[23]

It has further been related from him that he declared: "*Zuhd* is to do without meeting people."

I said: "And this is an allusion by him to seclusion and (concealed) devotional worship, as well as finding friendly solace in loneliness."

Abū Sulaymān al-Khaṭṭābī 🙵 has indeed excelled when he said:

> I found solacing friendliness in my loneliness, and clang to my house
> That way amiable friendliness endured, and happiness increased
> Time has disciplined me, and I don't mind
> I fled, so I'm neither visited nor do I visit
> I will not ask anyone for favors so long as I'm alive
> whether the sitting companion departs or the governor travels away.

And Manṣūr the jurist said excellently as well:

> Good gathers better in silence and in clinging to one's houses
> So if this or that is equal for you, then be contented with the least food.

In the same vein are the words of the judge Abū Bakr b. al-ʿArabī:

> A Muslim attains untainted safety
> when he repairs to a dwelling and some basic nourishment
> What then is slowed down and deferred
> after he takes shelter in a house and a minimum modicum of food?

Poems on this abound. Abū Muṭīʾ Makḥūl b. al-Faḍl al-Nasafī put it well when he said:

> Trace a path, O self, so that I aim at an Absolute One,
> Everlasting Sustainer of All, Sustaining Himself on none
> And leave me alone, lest I seek anyone other than my Lord
> He is my full sufficiency and my friendly companion, so forgo people
> In none apart from Him will you ever find any refuge.

Jaʿfar b. Sulaymān stated the following: I asked a woman about the devout worshippers, and said to her: "Who is with you in your house?" She replied: "The One I confide intimately with is my company. Can I experience loneliness once He is my intimate friend, ʿAbdallāh?"[24]

Al-Fuḍayl said: "Whenever I see the night approaching I rejoice in it, and say to myself that I will withdraw in the company of my Lord. Conversely, whenever I see that daylight has dawned upon me, I say *innā lillāhi wa innā ilayhi rājiʿūn* as if a calamity has struck me, out of dislike of meeting people, and the thought that someone who will engross me away from My Lord, Mighty and Exalted is He, will appear."[25]

It has also been said: "No one exercises *zuhd* [26] until and unless renouncing the World is dearer to him than appropriating it." That was said by Ibrāhīm b. Adham. I say: Such a saying concurs with the linguistic signification of *zuhd* in accordance with what has been stated hereabove.[27] One man said to al-Ḥasan:[28] "Our jurists say," [and before he could complete the sentence] al-Ḥasan remarked: "And have you seen any jurist (*faqīh*)? The *faqīh* is the one who practices *zuhd* in his worldly life, who possesses insightful knowledge of his *dīn*, and who persistently worships his Lord."Some said: "*Zuhd* is to do without in this world with one's heart." That was stated by Ibn al-Mubārak. I say: "This is a very good statement, since it is the same whether this world yields itself to his hand or not, as *zuhd* is one of the actions of the heart."

Likewise with the companions: This world fell into their hands, while they turned away from it with their hearts, in accordance with what shall be explained hereunder.

One group affirmed: *Zuhd* is love of death. I say: "This statement encompasses the semantic range of all the sayings quoted about it, as love of death implies love of meeting the Master as well as turning away from this World, so it represents the summit of all such sayings."[29]

The Prophet ﷺ explained *zuhd* with a clarification dispensing with any other statement on it. Ibn Mājah reported in his *Sunan*, and al-Tirmidhī in his *Jāmiʿ*,[30] on the authority of Abū Dharr al-Ghifārī ؓ that he narrated: The Messenger of Allāh ﷺ said:

> *Zuhd* in this World is not by forbidding to oneself the lawful or in dissipating wealth away. Rather, *zuhd* in this World is not to feel more confident in what is in your hand compared to what is in Allāh's hand ﷻ and to desire the reward of a calamity when you are afflicted by it more than you would do if it were to be held back for your sake and deferred.[31]

Ibn Mājah said: Hishām b. ʿAmmār stated the following: "Abū Idrīs al-Khawlānī used to mention that this hadith[32] was, among the *aḥādīth*, the equivalent of pure gold from within the family of golden products." Al-Tirmidhī said about it: "A strange (*gharīb*) hadith."[33] The name of Abū Idrīs al-Khawlānī was ʿĀ'idhullāh b. ʿAbdallāh. As for ʿAmr b. Wāqid[34] (found in the transmission chain of the said hadith), he was one whose narrations were disowned.[35]

I say: In this hadith, he ﷺ allusively indicated two vast dimensions: 1) reliance (on Allāh).[36] Reference to it has already occurred here above; and 2) contentment,[37] which falls into two types:

First is general contentment. It is to find no Lord but Allāh, no *dīn* but Islām, and no Messenger but Muḥammad. The *zuhd* of (general) contentment is something no Muslim is devoid of, since no profession of the *dīn* of Islām is true without it. That is the import of his statement ﷺ: "[Only] he who is pleased with Allāh as Lord, with Islām as *dīn*, and with Muḥammad as Messenger, is the one who tastes the flavor of *īmān*."[38] Muslim, *inter alia*, has reported it;

Second is specific contentment. It is the one spoken about by the masters of hearts.[39] The best expression of it came in the statement of al-Thawrī: "It is the hearts' happiness on the unfolding of the Decree." This second category is what the Prophet ﷺ alluded to in this hadith [from Abū Dharr], and Allāh knows best. This [narrower, more specific] variety is the ultimate goal of contentment: The slave manifests tolerant endurance of suffering at the inception of hardship; he is pleased with Allāh's reward as a quid pro quo for what He took away from him; and he resents nothing, hence does not reject the Decree. Shaqīq said: "I purchased a watermelon for my mother, who got angry when she cut it open. I said: 'Mother, what are you angry about? Do you reject the Decree? Or do you blame the ploughman or its seller, or perhaps you blame its Creator? As for the ploughman and the vendor, by Allāh, no sin can be attached to either of them, since they only wished it to be a watermelon of the best quality. In truth, I see you blaming none but its Creator, so fear Allāh and do not blame

Him.'" Shaqīq went on to state: "By Allāh, my mother never heard from me a more beneficial talk than that." Al-Zubayr b. Bakkār said: "ʿAlī b. Muḥammad b. ʿAbdallāh related to me the following: Ghaylān wrote to one of his brothers who had been stricken by a calamity that befell his son: 'Allāh granted you the gift of your son, and imposed on you the duty of educating him and providing for him, while you feared the testing of your faith by means of your son, whereupon your happiness was strengthened by such gift. When Allāh retracted the gift of his life, removed from you the task of disciplining him, and you thereby became safe from his trial, your fretful despondency grew stronger. [If only you exercised patience vis-à-vis such testing affliction],[40] you would have delighted in the loss you consoled yourself about. When this writing of mine reaches you, bear patiently the matter with the reward for which you cannot dispense, and the punishment of which you cannot endure, and know that every calamity that causes you to rejoice with the reward does not banish the grief it encompasses, that is the everlasting grief. Peace.'"

CHAPTER 2 (29)

SOVEREIGNTY OVER THIS WORLD AND EXERCISING *ZUHD* THEREIN

They are three things: curbing hope; mentioning death; and visiting the graves. Al-Bukhārī reported from (ᶜAbdallāh) Ibn ᶜUmar that he said: The Messenger of Allāh ﷺ took me by my shoulder and said: "Be in the *dunyā* as if you were a stranger or a traveller crossing it."[41] Ibn ᶜUmar used to say: "If you enter the evening, do not wait for the morning, and if you enter the morning, do not wait for the evening. Moreover, take from your time of wealth what benefits your time of sickness, and from your life what avails you in death." It has been narrated from ᶜAbdallāh b. ᶜUmar that he said: The Messenger of Allāh ﷺ passed by us while we were attending to a hut of ours. He ﷺ said: "What is this?" We replied: "Its foundation has become weak, so we are busy putting it right." He thus commented: "I do not see the matter (of death) but that it is more urgent than that."[42] Al-Tirmidhī said: Ḥadīth *ḥasan ṣaḥīḥ*.[43]

Ibn Mājah reported on the authority of Abū Ayyūb that he said: A man came to the Messenger of Allāh ﷺ and said: "O Messenger of Allāh, teach me concisely." He ﷺ replied: "If you rise for prayer, pray like the man who is bidding farewell (to this World), do not talk with words you are going to apologize for, and gather despair about what is in the hands of people."[44] It has already been mentioned before.[45]

He [Ibn Mājah] further reported on the authority of [ᶜAbdallāh] Ibn Masᶜūd that the Messenger of Allāh ﷺ said: "I used to forbid you to visit the graves before. Visit them now, since they stimulate *zuhd* in this World and make one remember the Afterlife."[46] Wuhayb b. al-Ward stated the following: "Nūḥ ﷺ built a house made of reeds. It was said to him: 'If only you had built a different type of house!' He replied: 'That is a lot for one who is going to die.'"[47] Ibn al-Muhājir said: "Nūḥ ﷺ spent 950 years among his nation in a house built of hair." They said: "O Prophet of Allāh, why did you not build something other than that?" He replied: "I am going to die today, (or) I am going to die tomorrow."

Al-Tirmidhī reported on the authority of ʿAbdallāh [like that in the Arabic text of al-Tirmidhī's work, without qualification] that he said: The Messenger of Allāh ﷺ stood on a mat and the traces of it appeared on his side. We thus said: "O Messenger of Allāh, what if we get for you some soft bedding and a nice carpet you can sleep on?" He ﷺ replied: "What have I got to do with the *dunyā*! I am but a rider who takes shade under a tree, then departs and leaves it behind."[48]

The one who said the following has excelled:

Donate this World away, it will be driven to you spontaneously
Isn't vanishing the final destination of it?
Your World is like nothing but a shade
then permission is given to depart.

Another one said, likewise excellently:

Seek this World with eagerness and haste
This World is only like a shifting shade
We are in it akin to a travelling party alighting
It is said that as soon as such party establishes itself it moves away without fail.

Our men of knowledge stated: The matter being like that, it does not befit a person endowed with intellect to be deceived by this World. Truthful are the words of the one who affirmed:

Dreams during sleep or like a withdrawing shade
Surely the judicious person is not duped by the like thereof.

Ibn ʿAbbās transmitted from the Prophet ﷺ that he said: "If you wish to attain what is with Allāh ﷻ, be in this world as guests stopping over for a limited while."[49]

Manṣūr[50] narrated from al-Ḥasan that he said: "When death came upon Salmān,[51] he wept, so it was said to him: 'O Abā ʿAbdallāh,[52] what makes you weep given that you are a companion of the Messenger of Allāh ﷺ ?' He said:

'For myself, I do not weep in grief for the departing *dunyā*. Rather, the Messenger of Allāh ﷺ entered into a covenant with us, and I discarded his covenant. He ﷺ solemnly stipulated that the sufficient provision of any one of us should be the provision of a rider.' Manṣūr said: When he passed away, they had a look and, lo! they found approximately thirty silver coins left in his possession."[53]

Thābit narrated from Anas that Saʿd (Ibn Abī Waqqāṣ) visited him in his sickness and said to him [Salmān]: "What makes you weep, brother?" The aforementioned narration then follows. It has been reported by Ibn Mājah in his *Sunan*, saying therein: Thābit mentioned: "It reached me that he left behind no more than some twenty silver coins from a disbursement to him."[54]

Al-Tirmidhī narrated the following: Maḥmūd b. Ghaylān[55] related to us: ʿAbd al-Razzāq informed us: Sufyān informed us from Manṣūr and al-Aʿmash from Abū Wā'il that he said: Muʿāwiyah[56] came to Abū Hishām b. ʿUtbah[57] on a visit to him while he was sick. He said to Abū Hishām: "Uncle, what is causing you to weep? A pain that is disquieting you, or a desire for the *dunyā*?" He replied: "Neither of the two. Rather, the fact that the Messenger of Allāh ﷺ concluded a covenant with us which I did not abide by. He ﷺ had said 'A servant, and a riding beast in the path of Allāh, is all that suffices you[58] in terms of gathered wealth,'[59] yet today I find in my house that I have gathered [wealth in excess of that]." Ibn Mājah, too, reported it, and it is authentic [*ṣaḥīḥ*].

CHAPTER 3 (30)

THE VIRTUE OF *ZUHD* AND ITS FRUIT

Ibn Mājah reported on the authority of Sahl b. Saᶜd al-Sāᶜidī that he said: A man came to the Messenger of Allāh ﷺ and said: "Messenger of Allāh, guide me to an action Allāh will love me for if I do it, and I will be loved for it by people, too." The Prophet ﷺ replied: "Do without[60] in the *dunyā*, and Allāh will love you. And do without what is in the hands of people, people will then love you."[61]

He [Ibn Mājah] further reported on the authority of Abū Khallād, to whom some companionship of the Prophet ﷺ is attributed, that he said: The Messenger of Allāh ﷺ said: "If you see the man who has been gifted *zuhd* and great parsimony in speech, draw near him, since he is made to acquire knowledge."[62]

ᶜAbdallāh b. Masᶜūd said: "Today you perform more prayers and carry out heavier acts of worship than the companions of the Messenger of Allāh ﷺ yet they were better than you." They asked: "And why is that so?" He replied: "They exercised greater *zuhd* in the *dunyā*, and were more desirous of the Other World than you."

Sufyān al-Thawrī stated: "If the slave does without in this life, Allāh entrenches wisdom firmly in his heart, makes his tongue express such wisdom, empowers him to discern the defects of his self, and turns the sickness of his self into the cure of his self."

CHAPTER 4 (31)

STATES OF THOSE WHO PRACTISED *ZUHD* IN THIS WORLD

Their [states] are six: 1) Speech; 2) Attire; 3) Food; 4) Patient bearing of poverty and a needy state; 5) Refraining from asking; and 6) Obscurity (self-effacement).

1. SPEECH

As for *speech*, which is the first of such states, it is the topmost goal, by achieving concordance between what one says and what one does. Allāh ﷻ has indeed censured in His Book a nation accustomed to command righteous actions they themselves did not carry out, and said therein: *Do you order people to devoutness and forget yourselves, when you recite the Book? Will you not use your intellect?* (2:43).[63]

Manṣūr the jurist put it well as follows:

> A people who enjoin
> what they themselves do not implement
> are verily madmen, even though they might not go mad
> in an ordinary clinical sense.

Whereas Abū al-ʿAtāhiyah stated:

> You described *taqwā* as if you yourself were endowed with it
> Yet the odor of misdeeds from your clothes is spreading
> How ugly is the urging to *zuhd* by the preacher
> who sets people upon *zuhd* without him practising it

Were he in his prompting to *zuhd* veracious,
the mosque would be his house morning and evening
If the people reject, why is it that he
asks the people for favors and does not lie down?[64]
Divine provision is distributed on recipients you are not oblivious to
Both the fair-skinned and the dark-skinned strive after it.

And Abū al-Aswad al-Duʿalī excellently wrote:

Don't forbid creation while you engage in something similar
[That is] a huge blemish, if you do so
Begin with your self, and command it away from straying
for, if it stops such straying, you are indeed a wise man
Then if you admonish, your counsel is accepted,
the speech emanating from you is used as a model to guide behavior,
and teaching (others) yields benefits.

Ibrāhīm al-Nakhaʿī said: I strongly abhor story-telling because of three verses (of the Qur'ān): a) His Statement ﷻ: *Do you order people to devoutness and forget yourselves?* b) His other statement ﷻ: *You who have iman! Why do you say what you do not do?* (61:2);[65] c) as well as His statement ﷻ: *I would clearly not want to go behind your backs and do something I have forbidden you to do* (11:88).[66]

II. DRESS

Rāfiʿ b. Thābit ﷺ looked at the ruler of al-Kūfah who was busy preaching. He said: "Have a look at your ruler who preaches to the people while wearing the clothes of the sinful." He had in fact soft clothes on him.

III. FOOD

It should be of a median type. These three states are reciprocally attesting, each of them verifying the trueness of the other.

IV. PERSEVERANCE

His patient self-restraint in the face of neediness and poverty, if it occurs or befalls him, whereupon no trace thereof becomes visible on him, in the way He ﷻ described such type of people by His statement: *The ignorant consider them rich because of their reticence* (2:272).[67] This is the mark by which they are known. It is their satisfaction with the judgment of the Master. It has also been said that what is meant by *al-taʿaffuf* is not reticence but self-adornment or beautifying (*al-tajammul*), just as He ﷻ said: *Therefore be patient with a patience which is beautiful* (70:5).[68] It has further been said that he gives preference to others over himself, so that the giver who bestowed something on him develops the illusion that he is rich. Another interpretation is that it means not to store anything out of fear of the future, as well as not to ask anyone save Allāh ﷻ in the same way that the righteous slave said: *My Lord, I am truly in need of any good You have in store for me* (28:24).[69] The meaning thereof is: I am truly in need of my provision which You have written for me, so if it is (thus written), send it to me and remove my need. I said: This last one is the best of such statements regarding the aforementioned, Allāh willing, since by it he causes his need to lodge in the will of Allāh ﷻ while he displays self-adornment to his fellow human beings who accordingly regard him as rich. The one who said the following has spoken well:

> My friend asks me what my state is
> Self-sufficiency has deluded him, though I toiled and strove.

The quotation of this verse has occurred previously in this work.[70] Another one said (and mention thereof, too, is found in an earlier passage of this book):[71]

> I ennoble my face above directing it, when putting forward a request, to other than the One, the Everlasting Sustainer.

The judge Abū Bakr b. al-ʿArabī said: "One of the Sufis forbade asking,[72] declaring it to be a repulsive and ignominious condemnation of the Lord on the part of the slave. This is far-reaching ignorance. Allāh has verily informed us that His slaves encompass both the poor and the rich man, commanding us in the process to visit the poor often. That is from His judgment and from His wisdom alike. What reviling condemnation is there in the needy man informing us about his state that He has singled him by, given that Allāh ﷻ has acquainted us with such state generically (by apprising us of the mixture of rich and poor among His slaves)?"

They have said: "In it one detects self-debasement by a man."[73] We replied thereto: "What debasement is entailed by your Master assigning a blessing He has bestowed upon you to your brother's hand, which blessing He has stored in him for you (so that you receive it indirectly from his hand)? Self-lowering lies in the asking, not in the one who asks. The addressee is your storing treasurer:

If he gives you what he has been commanded with, he will be rewarded, and if he dislikes (doing that) or wavers (about it), he will be recompensed with a wrongdoing written against his name."

They have also said: "In it there is harm inflicted to the one who is asked, since, if he grants the request generously, parting with his wealth weighs heavily on him, and, if he stints in it, that is a blameworthy image (which he projects of himself)." To this we said in reply: "Allāh placed a heavy burden on them[74] yet they were not stingy with the favor Allāh regaled them with, deeming it to be good for them whereas it was bad for them." In support of their stance they have narrated a hadith from the Prophet ﷺ: "Asking people is one of the shamelessly loathsome acts."[75] We said as a response to them: "Narrating this hadith is actually one of the most impudently detestable acts, one of the biggest major sins, and one of the gravest offences."

V. SUFFICIENCY

If he has what suffices him he should not ask Allāh for other than one day's food. That is in accordance with the hadith of Sahl b. al-Ḥanẓaliyyah, which has been quoted before.[76]

VI. SELF-CONCEALMENT

This is to be unknown through self-concealment, which conforms to what is found in the hadith of Abū Umāmah[77] from the Prophet ﷺ:

> Verily, the most fortunate of my friends in my judgment, and the one with the best final destiny, is a believer whose social state is slight, who possesses his lot in prayer, whose worship of his Lord is the best, who obeys Him the most in secrecy, and who is obscure among people, no fingers pointing (attentively) at him.[78]

Mention of the hadith has already occurred before.[79] Uways al-Qaranī said to ʿUmar (b. al-Khaṭṭāb): "It is dearer to me if you let me be among the poor and needy people." Muslim has reported it [in his *Ṣaḥīḥ*]. If the righteous people were recognized they used to flee the way Uways did, for he hurriedly went away and proceeded on his path as soon as he was noticed.

CHAPTER 5 (32)

THE PROPHET'S *ZUHD*

In this chapter mention will be made, by way of a sample, of some aspects of the Prophet's *zuhd* ﷺ in his livelihood, food, attire, and transport. It has been quoted earlier that in Abū Umāmah's hadith he said ﷺ "My Lord offered me the land of Makkah in its gold and silver equivalent. I said: No, Lord," etc.[80]

In Muslim's *Ṣaḥīḥ* one finds on the authority of Abū Dharr (al-Ghifārī) that he said: I was walking early at night with the Prophet ﷺ in the section of al-Madīnah paved with black stone,[81] and we were looking at (the mountain of) Uḥud, whereupon the Messenger of Allāh ﷺ said to me: "O Abā Dharr!" I said: "At your command, Messenger of Allāh!" He said: "What gladdens me is that this mountain of Uḥud be gold with me and three nights should pass, and out of it there is left with me, after the lapse of such period, no gold coin but one coin which I would set aside and keep ready to pay debt. What delights me is to spend it (all) among the slaves of Allāh like this (and he pointed by his noble hand in front of him), like this (pointing thereby to his right side), and like this (pointing on his left side)."[82] Al-Bukhārī, too, reported it.

Al-Tirmidhī reported on the authority of Abū Umāmah that he said: "Not even a loaf of barley bread used to be left over (for storage and future consumption) in the household of the Messenger of Allāh ﷺ."[83] (He commented: Ḥadīth *ḥasan ṣaḥīḥ*).

In the following narration from (ʿAbdallāh) Ibn ʿAbbās he said: "The Messenger of Allāh ﷺ used to sleep for consecutive nights hungry,[84] his family unable to find something to give him for supper. The bulk of the bread he ate was made of barley."[85] Al-Tirmidhī commented: Ḥadīth *ḥasan ṣaḥīh*.

It has been narrated from Sahl b. Saʿd (al-Sāʿidī) that he was asked: "Did the Messenger of Allāh ﷺ use to eat (bone) marrow?" Sahl replied: "The Messenger of Allāh ﷺ never saw the bone marrow until he met Allāh ﷺ." He was further asked: "Did you use to have sieves during the time of the Messenger of Allāh ﷺ?" He said: "We had no sieves." The question was thus posed: "How did you manage to make use of barley then?" He answered: "We used to puff it in the air (with our own hands or mouths) following its grinding, and after the evaporation of whatever residue was left in the sieve, we would strew it [moisten it with water we would sprinkle on it] and then knead it."[86] Al-Tirmidhī said about it: Ḥadīth *ṣaḥīh*.[87] Ibn Mājah, too, reported it in his *Sunan*.

Ibn Mājah further reported on the authority of Umm Ayman that she sifted flour and prepared with it a loaf of bread for the Prophet ﷺ. He said: "What is this?" She replied: "It is a meal we make in our region, so I loved to prepare a loaf of it for you." He said: "Return it thereto, then knead it."[88]

And it has been narrated from ʿĀ'ishah رضي الله عنها that she said: "From the time he arrived in al-Madīnah to the day when he passed away, the family of Muḥammad ﷺ never ate a meal made of wheat to their fill three nights in a row."[89] In another transmission it is said: "The family of Muḥammad ﷺ never ate barley bread to their fill for any two consecutive days,right through until he passed away."[90] In yet another narration we find: "[b]arley bread, save that one of such two days only dates would be eaten."[91]

Al-Bukhārī reported that ʿĀ'ishah رضي الله عنها said: "Until he met Allāh ﷻ the family of Muḥammad ﷺ never ate wheat bread with condiment for two days in succession."[92]

And from her as well رضي الله عنها it is narrated that she said: "When the Messenger of Allāh ﷺ passed away, my shelf was empty of anything which a human being could eat save for a half piece of barley in one shelf of mine. I ate some of it, then it stayed by me for a long time, and when I tried to weigh it one day, lo! it had all but come to nought."[93] Both al-Bukhārī and Muslim reported it.

I said: ʿĀ'ishah has informed you, my readers, of what was the daily livelihood of the Prophet ﷺ stemming from his *zuhd* in this World, despite the continuous succession of military conquests, and the cornucopia of wealth and collected taxes and levies flowing [to him].

In the *Ṣaḥīḥayn* (of al-Bukhārī and Muslim) we find, again from her that the Messenger of Allāh ﷺ bought food to be paid on a later date from a Jew, and gave him in pledge for the purchase price thereof his iron coat of armor.[94] Al-Nasā'ī reported the hadith of (ᶜAbdallāh) Ibn ᶜAbbās ﷺ that he said: "The Messenger of Allāh ﷺ passed away while his armor was pawned to a Jew in exchange for 30 double-handed scoops of barley [he purchased] for his family."[95]

Ibn Mājah reported on the authority of Abū Hurayrah that he said: "One day the Messenger of Allāh ﷺ was given some hot meal and he ate [it]. When he finished it he said: 'Allāh's is the praise! No hot meal had entered my stomach since such-and-such a time.'"[96]

It has been narrated from ᶜUrwah b. al-Zubayr that he said: My maternal aunt said to me: "By Allāh, my son, we spent 40 nights and no fire nor lamp was lighted in the house of the Messenger of Allāh ﷺ throughout that sojourn. He [ᶜUrwah b. al-Zubayr] said: 'I then asked her: In such a case, what did you use to live by?' She replied: 'The two black things, dates and water, nothing else.'"[97]

ᶜĀ'ishah ﷺ said: "By Allāh, we verily used to wait for the (new) crescent, and then the next crescent, and then the next, three crescents in two months, and no fire was lighted throughout that period in the house of the Messenger of Allāh ﷺ.[98] Muslim reported it.

[Abū Bakr Aḥmad b. Muḥammad b. Isḥāq b. al-Sanī, the *ḥāfiẓ* of hadith,[99] narrated the following: "Aḥmad b. Maḥmūd al-Wāsiṭī informed us saying: ᶜAbd al-Karīm b. al-Haytham related to us: ᶜUbayd b. Yaᶜīsh related to us: Yūnus b. Bukayr related to us: Saᶜīd b. Maysarah related to us from Anas b. Mālik from Abū al-Dardā' that he said: the Messenger of Allāh ﷺ did not use to sift out the flour, and he only had one shirt.][100]

It has been reported from the hadith of Hishām b. ᶜUrwah from his father from ᶜĀ'ishah ﷺ that she said: "The Messenger of Allāh ﷺ did not take for him anything in pairs, whether two shirts or two cloaks[101] or two loincloths, save for two sandals."[102]

Al-Aḥnaf b. Qays heard ᶜUmar b. al-Khaṭṭāb ﷺ say to Ḥafṣah: "I ask you in the name of Allāh, taking an oath by Him in your reply thereto: Are you aware that the Messenger of Allāh ﷺ used to put his clothes aside to be washed, Bilāl would then come to him and recite the call to the prayer to him, and he would find no clothing which he could wear to the prayer until the said clothes had dried and he was able to go out dressed in them?"

Al-Bukhārī reported from ʿĀ'ishah ﷺ that she said: "The bedding which the Messenger of Allāh ﷺ used to sleep on was a skin stuffed inside with palm-fibers."[103] Ibn Mājah, too, reported it, though the Arabic word for "bedding" in his narration was given by him as *ḍijā'* instead of *firāsh*.[104] It[105] has been narrated by al-Bukhārī, too.

Al-Tirmidhī reported from her[106] that she said: "The pillow which the Prophet ﷺ used to recline on was made of skin with fibers in its interior."[107] He said about it: Hadith *ḥasan ṣaḥīḥ*.

As for Abū Dāwud, he reported the following: "Musaddad related to us: Hammād related to us from Khālid al-Ḥadhdhā' from Abū Qilābah from one of the family members of Umm Salamah[108] that he said: "The bedding of the Messenger of Allāh ﷺ was similar to what a deceased person is made to lay on in his grave, and the *masjid* used to be by the side of the bed where he would lean on with his head."[109]

Ibn Mājah reported the following: ʿAmr b. Rāfiʿ related to us: Jarīr related to us from Muslim (b. Kaysān) al-Aʿwar from Anas b. Mālik that he said: "The Messenger of Allāh ﷺ used to visit the sick frequently, escort the deceased to their final resting places, answer the invitation of the slave, and ride a donkey. On the day of (Banū) Qurayzah and al-Naḍīr[110] he was riding a donkey. On the day of Khaybar he was seated on a donkey muzzled by a halting rope of bast, and underneath him was a pack-saddle made of fibers, too."[111]

In the *Ṣaḥīḥayn* (of al-Bukhārī and Muslim) we encounter the following narration from Muʿādh b. Jabal to the effect that he said: "I was riding at the rear of the Messenger of Allāh ﷺ seated on a donkey by the name ʿUfayr, etc."[112] Muslim reported it.

CHAPTER 6 (33)

ZUHD OF THE COMPANIONS

I n this present chapter mention will be made, (also) by way of a concise specimen, of some aspects of the companions' *zuhd* 🌿.

I) We start with ABŪ BAKR AṢ-ṢIDDĪQ 🌿. One of the jurists examined al-Shiblī by means of the following question (on the rules of *zakāt*): "Shaykh, how much is levied on the one possessing five camels?" Al-Shiblī asked him: "According to our *madhhab* or according to yours?" He said: "Why, have you got a *madhhab* different from ours?" Al-Shiblī replied: "Yes." He asked: "And which one is it?" Al-Shiblī answered: "Well, in terms of your *madhhab*, the tax on such property is one sheep from his livestock.[113] As for our *madhhab*, the whole of such property is given out to you." He said: "Have you an imam you follow in this *madhhab*?" Al-Shiblī replied: "Yes, the Commander of the Believers Abū Bakr al-Ṣiddīq 🌿 since he brought his entire wealth to the Prophet 🌼 and the Prophet 🌼 asked him: 'What did you leave for your dependents?' whereupon he replied: 'Allāh and His Messenger.'"[114]

During the illness of which he died he said: "I saw this world come before me and it genuflected, but it refrained from approaching me further.[115] Surely a day will come when you will adorn yourselves with silk drapes and water basins of silk brocade, keeping your distance in the process from woollen beds,[116] and yet you (once) got to the point where you used to find yourselves in the most severe condition, nibbling on the forage of thorny plants [being anxiously disquieted and restlessly fidgety].[117] I swear to Allāh: That one of you be brought forward and beheaded without having perpetrated anything deserving of such a penalty being prescribed for him; this would be better for him than to float in the flood of this World."[118]

He was once asked: "O caliph of the Messenger of Allāh ﷺ why do you not utilize the people of Badr (for political offices)?" He replied: "I am aware of their status, but I dislike to soil them by this world.[119]

II) As for ᶜUMAR IBN AL-KHAṬṬĀB ؓ he brought half of his wealth, and kept the remaining half for his dependents. He wore a new shirt, then asked for a blade and said to his son [ᶜAbdallāh]: "Son, trim the (long) sleeve(s) of the shirt. Place your forefingers across the edge of my knuckles and clip the balance hanging out." ᶜAbdallāh said: "I clipped the two sleeves on both sides of the shirt, but some part of the sleeves protruded out on another."[120] I [ᶜAbdallāh] said: "Father, what if I put the trim right with a pair of scissors?"[121] ᶜUmar replied: "My son, (no, it is fine, for) I have seen the Messenger of Allāh ﷺ do it that way."

He kept on wearing his shirt like that, until it fell apart [ᶜAbdallāh further narrated], and oftentimes I used to notice the fallen threads hanging over his feet.[122]

Al-Ḥasan[123] said: "ᶜUmar ؓ gave a *khuṭbah* while he was the caliph wearing a loincloth with twelve patches on it."[124]

Qatādah said: "It has been mentioned to us that ᶜUmar ؓ said: "If I wanted, I would eat the most pleasant food and wear the finest clothes from all of you, but I save my delights for the other world."[125]

Al-Aḥnaf b. Qays said: I heard ᶜUmar say: "I am the most knowledgeable of you about reducing the standard of living, but if I wished I would have the most pleasant life of all of you. By Allāh, I am not ignorant of (how to dress) a camel's humps,[126] of grilled meat, of *ṣināb* or *ṣalā'iq*, but I have chosen to spare my pleasures for the Hereafter. In describing a category of people, Allāh ﷻ has said: '*You dissipated the good things you had in your worldly life and enjoyed yourselves in it*' (46:19).[127]

The word *al-ṣilā'*, with the elongation of the ᶜ*alif* and the *kasrah* on the *ṣād*, means broiled meat. It has been so named because it is warmed by exposing it to the heat of the fire and by burning it therein [*yuṣallā* or *yuṣlā*]. As for *al-ṣināb*, they are the spicy condiments made of mustard [seeds] and raisins,[128] whereas the term *al-ṣalā'iq* [with the *ṣād*] signifies the varieties of long thin bread. *Salā'iq* with the *sīn*, instead, denotes legumes and their like that are cooked in boiling water. And Ḥafṣ b. al-ʿĀṣ mentioned the following: I used to have lunch with ʿUmar 🕮 partaking of bread, oil and vinegar, or bread, milk and meat cut into strips and dried.[129] The least common item of food we used to have was fresh meat. ʿUmar used to say: Do not sift out the flour, for the whole of it is nutritional food.

III) About ʿUTHMĀN IBN ʿAFFĀN 🕮, suffice it for your knowledge of his *zuhd* that he equipped the Army of Hardship[130] with 300 camels, their saddle blankets and saddles included. In addition, he brought 1,000 gold coins to the Prophet 🕮 [131] scattering such wealth before him, while he left an equal balance as a protection for the ummah, lest discord[132] spread among them.

He used to feed the people with the rulers' food while eating bread, vinegar, and oil when he retreated into[133] his private house.

ʿAbdallāh b. Shaddād said: "I saw ʿUthmān b. ʿAffān on a Friday wearing a loincloth from ʿAdan[134] valued at four or five silver coins (only), as well as a torn wrap from al-Kūfah."[135]

IV) Concerning ʿALĪ IBN ABĪ ṬĀLIB 🕮 the following was said by one of the reliable narrators:[136] "I visited ʿAlī in al-Khawranq[137] at a time when he was shivering under a threadbare garment made of rough fibers [he was wrapping himself up with to keep warm in the cold]." I said to him: "Commander of the Believers, Allāh has given you and the members of your household a share in this wealth,[138] and yet you do this to yourself?" He replied: "By Allāh, I have not deprived you people of any of your properties. This is simply my velvet shawl that I brought with me from my home [i.e., al-Madīnah]."[139]

He once purchased a shirt for some silver coins and wore it. It hung over all the way to his fingers, so he commanded that the excess be clipped from it.[140]

Ibn al-Nabbāḥ came to him and said: "The public treasury is filled to capacity with every kind of yellow and white [gold and silver]. On hearing that, ʿAlī 🕮 set out to the public treasury and, having reached it, he gathered all the eligible beneficiaries, whereafter he distributed the entire contents thereof among them, saying while he was doing that: 'O yellow, turn yellow, o white, be white, deceive someone other than me, here! take!' He kept on doing so until not a single gold or silver coin remained, then ordered that the (emptied) treasury be sprinkled and prayed two *rakᶜats* in it in the hope that it will testify in his favor on the Day of Rising."[141]

On one occasion he was brought a plate of *fālūdhaj* [a sweet made of flour and honey]; the man serving him placed it before him. He said [addressing the sweet]: "Your smell is good and appetizing, your color is nice and appealing, your flavor is pleasant, but I loath to (re)train myself to do what it was previously unaccustomed to."[142]

I said: "The *zuhd* of these caliphs did not stem from compulsion and necessity, rather, it was an act of free election on their part: The choice of the more virtuous state, a deed of self-abasement vis-à-vis Allāh ﷻ as well as an emulation of their Prophet ﷺ."

Al-Tirmidhī has indeed reported the narration by Sahl b. Muᶜādh from his father to the effect that the Messenger of Allāh ﷺ said: "Whoever renounces (new and nice) clothes out of humility to Allāh, though capable of affording them, Allāh will call out for him over the heads of the creatures, in order to give him the choice of wearing any garb of *imān* he prefers."[143] He commented: *Ḥadīth ḥasan.*

V) Al-Ḥasan[144] said: "**ṬALḤAH B. ᶜUBAYDILLĀH** ؓ [whom we are going to deal with now] sold a piece of land (which he owned) for 700,000 silver coins. He spent one sleepless night with such money kept in his house, out of fearful concern over it. When he woke up in the early morning, he distributed (all of) it among the destitute."[145] Ziyād b. Ḥudayr said: "I saw Ṭalḥah b. ᶜUbaydillāh distributing 100,000 silver coins among the people in the mosque."[146]

Whenever Abū Bakr used to mention the day of Uḥud he would say: "The whole of it was the day of Ṭalḥah."

VI) Turning to **AL-ZUBAYR B. AL-ᶜAWWĀM** ؓ he owned 1,000 slaves[147] who used to hand over to him the land taxes (they had collected). Each night he divided the entire amount they brought him, and by the time he had returned to his house none of it was left in his possession.[148] Imam Aḥmad b. Ḥanbal reported it.[149]He sold a house for 600,000.[150] It was said to him: "Abā ʿAbdallāh,[151] you have charged an immoderate price." He replied: "No, by Allāh, you shall come to know that I charged no exorbitantly excessive price, since all the proceeds of the sale are spent in the path of Allāh ﷻ."

On the day of the Battle of the Camel, he set about instructing his sons on what to do with his debts, saying: "Sons, if you lack the strength to do something, then seek the help of my Master in carrying it out." ʿAbdallāh b. al-Zubayr said: "I asked: And who is your master?" He said: "Allāh." Proceeding with his narration, ʿAbdallāh said: "I swear by Allāh, whenever I fell into some anxiety concerning his debts I only had to say: O Master of al-Zubayr, satisfy the debt of al-Zubayr, and He would immediately settle his debt."[152]

When al-Zubayr ﷺ was killed, he did not leave behind a single gold or silver coin. He only left two estates, one of them being al-Ghābah,[153] and eleven houses in Egypt. His debt derived from the fact that when someone came to him with goods and gave them to him for safekeeping, al-Zubayr would tell him not to do so, but rather to convert them into a loan, stating that he feared their extinction. ʿAbdallāh (b. al-Zubayr) went on to say: "I counted his debts and found that they amounted to one million and two hundred thousand."[154] ʿAbdallāh settled his debts for him from the legacy of the aforementioned properties, according to what al-Bukhārī has mentioned in his *Ṣaḥīḥ*.

ʿAbdallāh (b. al-Zubayr) attended the pilgrimage season for four years in a row summoning whoever had a credit over al-Zubayr to approach him. Once four years had elapsed, he divided his estate, and his heirs received the balance thereof. Al-Zubayr had four wives, and each one of them inherited one million and two hundred thousand (silver coins). His whole estate consisted of fifty million and two hundred thousand (silver coins).[155] Al-Bukhārī, *raḥimahullāh*, mentioned that.

VII) Lastly, ʿ**ABD AL-RAḤMĀN B. ʿAWF** ﷺ is one of the ten companions for whom the *jannah* has been (prophetically) attested to (in this World) ﷺ. ʿAbd al-Raḥmān migrated to Abyssinia and was involved in both migrations. He also took part in all the battles (during the prophetic era), and remained steadfast by the Prophet's side ﷺ on the day of Uḥud. The Messenger of Allāh ﷺ prayed one *rakʿah* behind him during the expedition of Tabūk, and he said ﷺ: "No

Prophet was taken away from this World before praying behind a righteous man of his nation." He was one of the affluent companions, his wealth having come entirely from trade.

Al-Zuhrī said: During the time of the Prophet ﷺ ʿAbd al-Raḥmān b. ʿAwf ﵁ gave out as *ṣadaqah* half of his wealth, 4,000, then gave another 40,000 gold coins in *ṣadaqah*, and subsequently financed 500 horses at first, followed by 100,000 horses in the path of Allāh, together with 100 riding camels.

Ownership of a caravan from Greater Syria,[156] comprising 700 riding camels, was handed over to him, and he turned it into a *ṣadaqah* in the path of Allāh, with their loads, saddles, and saddlebags included.[157]

In the book *al-Mustadrak* by al-Ḥākim, Abū ʿAbdallāh, Muḥammad b. ʿAbdallāh, we find from Jaʿfar b. Burqān that he said: "It has reached me that ʿAbd al-Raḥmān b. ʿAwf manumitted 30,000 families."[158] One comes across the following in the same book by al-Ḥākim: "ʿAbd al-Raḥmān used to be referred to as the apostle [*ḥawāriyy*][159] of the Messenger of Allāh ﷺ."[160] This narration, based on the hadith of Muḥammad b. Isḥāq, is authentic in accordance with the criterion of authenticity laid down by Muslim.

It has been narrated that ʿUmar b. al-Khaṭṭāb ﵁ used to visit Umm Kulthūm, the daughter of ʿUqbah, and ask her: "Did the Messenger of Allāh ﷺ tell you[161] to marry ʿAbd al-Raḥmān b. ʿAwf since he is the master of the Muslims?" She replied: "Yes."

It has further been narrated that ʿAlī ﵁ said to ʿAbd al-Raḥmān b. ʿAwf: I verily heard the Messenger of Allāh ﷺ say: "You are trustworthy in the eyes of the inhabitants of Heaven, and trustworthy in the eyes of the inhabitants of the Earth."[162]

I said: "ʿAbd al-Raḥmān b. ʿAwf, Allāh is pleased with him and may He please him, is one of the ten whose admission to *jannah* has been attested to [during their lifetime]. He is also one of the six whom ʿUmar and the companions of the Messenger of Allāh ﷺ appointed to determine among them the election of the new caliph. Of them, he was the one singled out for renouncing his lot of the caliphate, consequentially on his *zuhd*,[163] so that he could choose for the Muslims what Allāh had chosen for them. He gave his oath of allegiance to ʿUthmān, and by his allegiance the *bayʿah* to ʿUthmān was perfected.

The ummah was pleased with his role of trustworthy man, and the companions put him forward as an imam. The Messenger of Allāh ﷺ prayed one unit of prayer behind him, after he had commenced such *rakᶜah*, by joining his prayer behind him. He ﷺ performed no prayer behind any of the companions, with the exception of ᶜAbd al-Raḥmān and al-Ṣiddīq.

He is the one who acted by Allāh and for Allāh in his wealth in an appropriate manner. He is one of those about whom the Messenger of Allāh ﷺ said: "Save for those who spend their wealth this way and that,"[164] and so on and so forth about his praiseworthy qualities and laudable virtues.

Accordingly, no heed is paid to the narration to the effect that he will be the last to enter the Garden, and that he will crawl on the Day of Rising. I seek refuge in Allāh from conceiving of ᶜAbd al-Raḥmān crawling on the Day of Rising on account of his wealth and affluence.

Have you not taken note of what we mentioned earlier, that he is one of the ten, furthermore that he is one of the six whom the Messenger of Allāh ﷺ was pleased with when he passed away, one of the people of Badr, and one of the people of al-Ḥudaybiyyah? And such a man is going to crawl? I take shelter in Allāh from such an allegation!

Allāh ﷻ said: *Those of you who gave and fought before the victory are not the same* [as those who gave and fought afterwards] (57:10).[165] He also said ﷻ: *Allāh was pleased with the mu'minūn when they pledged allegiance to you under the tree...* (48:18). That is a sufficient virtue for you to consider.

In the second place, the hadith that they narrate (in support of their contention) has been transmitted by ᶜUmārah b. Zādān, about whom al-Bukhārī has said: "His hadith narration was often muddled."[166] Aḥmad (b. Ḥanbal) stated: "He narrates from Anas (b. Mālik) repudiated and disavowed *aḥādīth*." As for Ḥātim al-Rāzī, he said the following: "His hadith is not accepted as proof, whereas al-Dāraquṭnī asserted that he was weak."

Inter alia al-Muḥāsibī mentioned that when ᶜAbd al-Raḥmān died a group of the companions of the Messenger of Allāh ﷺ said: "We fear for ᶜAbd al-Raḥmān in connection with his proprietary legacy." Kaᶜb retorted: "What do you fear for him about? He earned wealth correctly, he spent it rightly, and he bequeathed it appropriately." Kaᶜb's comment came to the knowledge of Abū Dharr, who set out in anger looking for Kaᶜb. He took hold of a camel and then departed in search of Kaᶜb. Kaᶜb was told that Abū Dharr was after him, and so he fled away from where he was until he came to ʿUthmān (b. ʿAffān), recounting to him the story and pleading for his assistance. Abū Dharr, meanwhile, was approaching in hot pursuit of Kaʿb, unravelling the traces of Kaʿb's escape in the process. He eventually reached the house of ʿUthmān. As he entered it, Kaʿb went to sit behind ʿUthmān, fleeing away from Abū Dharr to such a shelter. Abū Dharr then said: "Son of a Jewess, you allege that what ʿAbd al-Rahmān left is unobjectionable and does not matter! The Messenger of Allāh ﷺ went out one day and said: 'The ones who have a lot are verily the ones who have little, save for those who spend (their wealth) in this [and that].'"[167]

Our people of knowledge, Allāh have Mercy on them, have said: "This is a false hadith which is not entrenched among narrations that are paid regard to. Its veracity is an impossibility, and it originates in the forgery of the ignorant."

Some of it has been narrated, but the route of transmission is disproved, because we find in the chain thereof Ibn Lahīʿah, who has been the target of critical assessments. Yaḥyā said: "His hadith is not accepted as proof."

Historical truth, moreover, teaches us that Abū Dharr died in the year 25 AH, whereas ʿAbd al-Raḥmān b. ʿAwf passed away in the year 31 AH, and thus lived seven years after Abū Dharr.

I said: What certifies ʿUmārah's forgery in the very narration we have quoted is his statement, ascribed to Abū Dharr: "Son of a Jewess!" This is an act of finding fault (with Kaʿb) on his part, for the like of which the Prophet ﷺ had previously rebuked him, as it is mentioned in Muslim's *Ṣaḥīḥ*, on Abū Dharr's authority, that he said: "A dispute arose between myself and one of my brothers (in the *dīn*), so I disgraced him by a reference to his mother, whereupon he complained about me to the Prophet ﷺ and he said: 'O Abā Dharr, you are a man in whom some *jāhiliyyah* lingers.'" I [Abū Dharr] said: "Messenger of Allāh ﷺ the wont of those reviling a man is to revile his father and mother." He said: "O Abā Dharr, you are a man in whom some *jāhiliyyah* lingers," etc.[168]

Can you countenance the possibility of Abū Dharr relapsing into the very thing the Prophet ﷺ reprimanded him about? That is preposterous to imagine in respect of someone of a lower status than him, so how much more far-fetched to attribute it to him, may Allāh be pleased with him and may He please him?

Likewise his statement (in the narration): "The ones who have a lot are verily the ones who have little, save for those who dispose of their wealth this way and that," is off the mark, given that ʿAbd al-Raḥmān b. ʿAwf is precisely one of those who spent it thus, in conformity with what we have mentioned hereabove.

To repeat, this hadith is a false one that the ignorant have forged.

As our people of knowledge have asserted, one does not direct any attention to it nor does he rely on it. Besides, ʿAbd al-Raḥmān b. ʿAwf is more virtuous than Abū Dharr by a long margin, due to his antecedence in Islam, and his inclusion in the ten for whom the Garden has been guaranteed in this world, which makes him one of the first ones to enter it, beating most of the rest into it, and one of those triumphant with such otherworldly reward. Anything other than that is given no consideration. Success and protection are by Allāh.

Additional elucidation of the aforementioned is to be found in the two chapters after this, Allāh ﷻ willing.

CHAPTER 7 (34)

THE VIRTUE OF ACQUIRING WEALTH PROPERLY AND SPENDING IT ON ITS RIGHTFUL BENEFICIARY

Al-Bukhārī reported on the authority of Abū Hurayrah that he said: The Messenger of Allāh ﷺ said: "This wealth is (like) sweet, succulently tender and fresh greenery: What an aid it is for the one who acquires it appropriately, and places it where it is due! As for he who appropriates it without rightful entitlement to it, he is like the one who eats without ever getting satiated."[169]

Muslim also reported on the authority of Abū Dharr (al-Ghifārī) from the Prophet ﷺ that he said: "The well-to-do will be the propertyless destitute on the Day of Rising, save for him on whom Allāh confers good [wealth], and he dispenses it to his right, left, in front of him and at his back, and who does good with it."[170] Al-Tirmidhī reported from Khawlah bint Qays, then under the authority of Ḥamzah b. ʿAbd al-Muṭṭalib ﷺ that she said: I heard the Messenger of Allāh ﷺ say: "This wealth is (like) sweet, succulently tender and fresh greenery: Whoever acquires it appropriately is blessed in it. By contrast, how many of those who hastily dispose of the wealth of Allāh and of His Rasūl according to the whims of their selves, who will get nothing but the Fire on the Day of Rising!"[171] Al-Tirmidhī said about it: This is a hadith *ḥasan ṣaḥīḥ*.

Al-Tirmidhī further reported on the authority of Abū Kabshah al-Anmārī that he mentioned that he heard the Messenger of Allāh ﷺ say: "Three attributes of character I swear by, and I relate to you a majestic saying which you should memorize." He said: "No slave's wealth is diminished by *ṣadaqah*; no slave is oppressed by an injustice which he bears patiently without Allāh increasing him in freedom from abasement; and no slave opens on his self a door of beseeching external help but that Allāh opens a door of poverty for him," or something like that. "And I (now) relate to you (another) statement, so commit it to memory from me. 'This World is but for four groups of people: [1] A slave on whom Allāh has bestowed wealth and knowledge, and he guards himself vis-à-vis Allāh in that, keeps ties with his family relatives by such dual gift, and recognizes Allāh's right in what He has provided him with of wealth and knowledge alike. This one is in the best of stations; [2] a slave whom Allāh has gifted with knowledge but not wealth, and who, his intention being truthful, says: If I had wealth, I would act with it as so-and-so who spends it in acts of goodness does. He is judged by his intention, and the reward for him and the one he would emulate (if only he possessed his means) are identical; [3] a slave on whom Allāh has conferred wealth without knowledge, who, in a state of ignorance, disposes of his wealth in the gratification of his self's caprices, does not fear Allāh concerning it, does not keep ties with blood relatives, and ignores Allāh's right in it. This one is in the lowest rank with Allāh; [4] and a slave whom Allāh has regaled with neither wealth nor knowledge, and this one says: If only I owned wealth I would act with it the same way as so-and-so (who spends it in evil pursuits). He is accorded the ruling of his intention, so his burden and the burden of the one he would emulate (were he granted the same means) are the same."[172] Al-Tirmidhī commented about it: Ḥadīth *ḥasan ṣaḥīḥ*.

Our people of knowledge, Allāh have Mercy on them, have said: "The import of this chapter has elucidated both the merit and demerit of wealth, and the fact that the owner thereof who spends it on what is right and places it where it rightfully belongs, is in the loftiest degrees and in the highest stations and upper chambers (in *jannah*)."[173] That is in conformity with what has been explicitly laid out in the Revelation, specifically in His statement ﷻ *It is not your wealth or your children that will bring you near to Us—only in the case of people who have* iman *and act rightly; such people will have a double recompense for what they did. They will be safe from all harm in the High Halls of Paradise* (34:37).

The Qur'ānic verses praising wealth are many, if one reads the Book of Allāh reflectively. That is a guideline creating in you the inducement to earn it, trade in it and gather it. Saᶜīd b. al-Musayyib used to say: There is no good in one who does not seek wealth, by which he discharges his debts and protects his honor and good repute, and which he leaves in inheritance to somebody else when he dies. The Messenger of Allāh ﷺ said to Saᶜd: "To leave your heirs rich is better than to leave them as indigent persons begging from people."[174] He ﷺ also said: "No wealth whatsoever benefited me more than Abū Bakr's wealth did."[175]

He ﷺ likewise said to ᶜAmr b. al-ᶜĀs: "How good is the wholesome wealth for the wholesome man."[176] He ﷺ made a prayer for Anas (b. Mālik), saying: "O Allāh, increase his wealth and offspring, and bless him in that."[177] All of this is firmly documented in the authentic *aḥādīth.*

At their death, Saᶜīd b. al-Musayyib left behind 400 gold coins, and Sufyān al-Thawrī, with all his *zuhd* and asceticism, 200. Sufyān al-Thawrī said about that: "To leave behind 10,000 silver coins which I am going to account for in the Reckoning is better to me than to be in want of people's help. He used to say as well: In this time, wealth is a weapon."

A man said to him: "O 'Abā ᶜAbdillāh,[178] do you retain this world in your grasp?" He replied: "Shut up, for if it were not for these golden coins those kings (out there) would cajole me and associate with me."[179]

Of the same import is the statement by ᶜAbd al-Raḥmān b. ᶜAwf: "How excellent is this wealth, by which I safeguard my honor and I extend to Allāh a good loan which He repays to me manifold times over its value!"

The (pious) predecessors never stopped praising wealth and gathering it for the sake of acts of kindness and benefaction such as grants and donations, and for the sake of assisting the poor. The majority of the companions earned wealth and bequeathed it on their deaths.[180]

In a narration, Abū Masᶜūd said: "The Messenger of Allāh ﷺ used to command that *ṣadaqah* be given out, whereupon one of us would set out at once and exert himself with toil and difficulty until he brought the *mudd* (a dry measure consisting of a handful of staple foodstuff). Nowadays, the least affluent of them possesses 100,000." Shaqīq said: He was alluding to himself.[181] This is a sound chain of transmission. Ibn Mājah reported it in his *Sunan* where he said: ᶜAbdallāh b. Numayr and Abū Bakr related to us, saying: Abū Usāmah related to us from Zā'idah from al-Aᶜmash [and the said narration then follows]. Muslim mentioned the narration in terms of its meaning, without reporting it literally.[182]

The consensus of learned opinions has settled on the permissibility of gathering wealth due to His statement ﷻ *So make full use of any booty you have taken which is halal and good* (9:70).[183] His other statement ﷻ: *[B]ut only by means of mutually agreed trade* (4:29), as well as His statement ﷻ: *You who have* imān*! give away some of the good things you have earned and some of what the earth produces for you* (2:266)[184] as well as other verses (of similar import).

Allāh ﷻ permitted the earning of wealth to establish a connection with Him and reach Him thereby, by fighting an enemy in warfare, assisting a poor man, feeding an orphan, helping someone oppressed or giving succor to one aggrieved and worried. So long as the sound intention in its acquisition is there, gathering it is more meritorious and virtuous (than its opposite), without any debate between the people of knowledge on that.

I said: This having been firmly entrenched, it points to the falseness of what they have mentioned and narrated, to the effect that ʿAbd al-Raḥmān b. ʿAwf will enter the Garden last and crawling. Their singling out ʿAbd al-Raḥmān b. ʿAwf in their concern is itself an indication of their ignorance, since they did not narrate the biographical accounts of the companions who left behind wealth, nor did they narrate the biographies of the pious predecessors who have set the guiding example. Were it not for fear of prolixity, we would have mentioned in that respect a great number of prophets, Allāh's blessings be on all of them, and other than them, may Allāh be pleased with them.

Al-Ṭabarānī, Sulaymān b. Aḥmad, reported the following: Muḥammad b. al-Faḍl al-Thaqafī related to us: Saʿīd b. Sulaymān al-Wāsiṭī related to us from Abū Usāmah[185] from Hishām b. ʿUrwah from his father that he said: "I got hold of Saʿd b. ʿUbādah while an announcer was calling out towards food: 'Whoever likes fat and meat should come to Saʿd.' Then I got hold of his son Qays inviting people loudly to what I mentioned. Saʿd b. ʿUbādah said: 'O Allāh, grant me praise, and grant me honor. There is no honor save by action, and no action save by wealth. O Allāh, little is not suitably wholesome for me, and I am not suitable for it.'"[186]

Suffice you what the utterly truthful one[187] said to his daughter ʿĀ'ishah ﵂ when death befell him: "By Allāh, after me no one is more loved than you, and no one is of mightier poverty than you."

CHAPTER 8 (35)

ELUCIDATION OF THE PROPHET'S STATEMENT ON HIS NATION'S TEST

This is an elucidation on the Prophet's ﷺ statement, "Every nation has its (peculiar) test, and the test of my nation is wealth,"[188] and Allāh's ﷻ statement, *Do not direct your eyes longingly to what We have given them to enjoy...* (20:129).[188]

Al-Tirmidhī reported on the authority of Kaᶜb b. ᶜIyāḍ that he said: I heard the Messenger of Allāh ﷺ say: "Every nation has its (peculiar) test, and the test of my nation is wealth."[190] He commented: This is a hadith *ḥasan ṣaḥīḥ gharīb*. Our people of knowledge, Allāh's Mercy be upon them, have said the following: "This is a report from him ﷺ informing us that all the nations have been subjected to a testing temptation. For some nations, it was a trial of their *tawḥīd* by the medium of idols which they worshipped, this one by the sun, that one by the moon, yet another one by the stars which they took as deities. Another nation, and they are the Jews, were tested by the presence of a prophet in their midst, ending up worshipping ᶜUzayr and declaring him to be the son of Allāh, while another group of them was tried by the calf which they devoted themselves to in worship. As for the Christians, they were tested by ᶜĪsā ﷺ. Some of them said: He is the God. Others said: He is the son of Allāh."

"For this ummah, He made the test lie in the gold and silver coins. As a result, love of wealth seized the majority of it, so that He ruffled for them the slavehood of the self-exalted and the conceited,[191] just as most nations were overwhelmed by the associationism (*shirk*) in the indirect causes spoiling their understanding of the Oneness of the Supreme Lord."[192]

I said: The aforementioned, together with what semantically resembles it, has been used as a supporting proof by those who disown gathering wealth, earning it, taking receipt of it and purchasing it, because of the corrupting vices stemming from that, and because of the good actions and the benefits which its owner is deprived of.

There is, however, no proof in it in their favor, since people's states in that regard differ, as unveiled by two Prophetic sayings:

1) The hadith of Abū Kabshah al-Anmārī quoted in the preceding chapter.

2) What has been reported by *inter alia* al-Bukhārī and Ibn Mājah on the authority of Abū Hurayrah that he said: The Messenger of Allāh ﷺ said: "Perish the slave of this World! Perish the slave of silver coins! Perish the slave of the black dress of silk fabric with embroidered markings! Perish the slave of the finely wrought velvet! If he is pricked by a thorn, he is unable to extract it with a chisel. Whenever he is given he is pleased, but if giving is withheld from him he becomes irate." Then he said about Thumāmah:[193] "Blessedness to a slave seizing the reins of his horse in the path of Allāh, his head dishevelled, his feet covered in dust. If he is appointed as sentinel, he is there guarding, and if he is assigned to directing the motion of the army, he is there at its rear protecting it. He seeks death on the spot. If he is given he thanks and if he is deprived he exercises patience."[194] Our people of knowledge have said that he ﷺ distinguished (therein) between the slave of wealth and passion and the slave sincerely devoted to his Master. He made a harsh supplication against the former with the purpose of reverting him to the Master, whereas He singled out the sincere one by the word *ḥabbadhā* (blessedness to),[195] which is the degree of His beloved friends. Evil is that wealth which engrosses away from the remembrance of Allāh and from the fulfilment of His rights. If it does not preclude that, such wealth is good, just as he said, Allāh's blessings and peace be upon him: "How good is the wholesome wealth for the wholesome man."[196]

Since, however, the safety and integrity of one's *dīn* is a rarity in the presence of wealth, and afflicting tests, together with corrupting calamities, get the upper hand (when wealth is owned), it has become mandatory to do with a little of it and flee from it, and it has become incumbent on a person to take such modicum of wealth that suffices him for his inescapable needs. The masters of understanding have said: "Whatever wealth or family connection distracts you away from Allāh is ill-omened for you."

Yaḥyā b. al-Mutawakkil said: "I was walking with Sufyān al-Thawrī when I passed by a man building an edifice and speaking in glowing terms of it. He (Sufyān al-Thawrī) said: 'Do not look at it, for he built it to be looked at.'"

Hishām b. ʿUrwah said: Whenever my father visited somebody possessed of some adornment of this World, he would hasten the return to his family and would stand by the door loudly reciting: *Do not direct your eyes longingly to what We have given certain of them to enjoy* to the end of the verse, whereafter he would exclaim: "Time for prayer! Time for prayer!" They would then rise and pray together.

CHAPTER 9 (36)

THE LOWLINESS OF THIS WORLD IN THE ESTEEM OF ALLĀH ﷻ

Al-Tirmidhī reported on the authority of Sahl b. Saᶜd [al-Sāᶜidī] that he said: The Messenger of Allāh ﷺ said: "Were this World in Allāh's esteem worth one wing of a mosquito, He would not have given a *kāfir* to drink one sip of water from it."[197] The following has been declaimed:

You hear from the passing days if you are resolute
for verily you lie in them between a proscribing and a mandating injunction
If this World preserved for a person his *dīn*
whatever has elapsed of them is not harmful
This World shall not equate a wing of a mosquito
nor the weight of a wing belonging to a flying creature
This World is not pleased as a recompense for a believer
nor is it satisfied to be the retribution for the unbeliever.

Muslim reported on the authority of Jābir b. ᶜAbdallāh that the Messenger of Allāh ﷺ passed by the market, entering it from one of its elevated sections. The people who were present gathered around him on both sides, and he walked by a dead young billy goat that had small ears. He got hold of its corpse and took it by one ear, whereupon he said: "Which of you would like to have this for a single silver coin?" They replied: "We do not like to have it for any sum whatsoever! And what are we going to do with it?" He said: "Would you like it to be yours?" They answered: "By Allāh, if it were alive, it would be a defective commodity because of its small ears, let alone now that it is dead." He said:

"And by Allāh, this World is certainly more contemptibly low in Allāh's esteem than this one (kid) is in yours."[198]

It has been narrated from the Prophet ﷺ that he said: "Part of this World's lowliness in the esteem of Allāh ﷻ lies in the fact that disobedience only takes place in it, and the fact that what is stored with Him is not attained save by renouncing it."[199]

Our people of knowledge have stated that the meaning of this World's baseness in Allāh's esteem is that He did not make it a goal in itself, sought after as such for its own sake, but rather a path taking one to other than itself; as well as the fact that He did not make it an abode of settlement and retribution, and only made it an abode of transit and trial. In addition, He granted it in the majority to the unbelievers and the ignorant, safeguarding the prophets, His friends and the *abdāl* [200] from it.

Suffice it for you, concerning its vileness in the esteem of Allāh, that He has belittled, disdainfully disparaged and censured it, and that He has loathed it, the lovers thereof and those devoted to it, being satisfied with nothing in it, for the person possessed of intellect, but desire-free devotional worship, critical reproaching thereof, and inflaming excitement to depart from it.

Notwithstanding its triviality, however, man cannot do without it since it is the intended path and the praiseworthy road. He said ﷺ: "Do not curse this World, for what a good riding animal it is for the believer! Good is attained by its medium, and through it one is rescued from evil."[201]

One man dispraised this World in the presence of ʿAlī b. Abī Ṭālib ﷺ whereupon ʿAlī said: "This World is an abode of truthfulness for the one who grasps its reality, an abode of salvation for the one who understands it, and an abode of richness for the one who takes his provision from it."

Maḥmūd al-Warrāq said in laudable verses:

> Do not follow the mention of this World and its passing time with censure
> if you suffer an adversity in it[202]
> Part of the nobility and virtue of this World
> is that the course of the Hereafter is made firmer by it.

To summarize: In every moment in time the slave has a state entailing either a praiseworthy or a blameworthy attribute. Judgments are connected to such attributes, and reward or punishment occasions from them. If good is found in this World in one respect only, it is something that cannot be dispensed with. The one who takes by the good aspect thereof, thus, will surely get good in return. This world is, after all, the riding beast of the wayfarer, the provision of the traveller, and the bridge of the passerby, not the abode of the purposeful voyager. It is the locus of the effort of the one who does with a little of it, hunting it and making use of it in moderation, without asking for a lot of it, and taking nourishment from it without hoarding. The simile of it is the sword, which suits the purpose of the just and the unjust man alike. Each of them disposes of it in accordance with his intention, and in conformity with what his will is enamored with. Whatever in this World brings closer to Allāh ﷻ and facilitates the worshipping of Him is the praiseworthy on every tongue, and the beloved to every man. The like of this is not cursed, nay, it is something desired and liked. An allusion to this is found in the use of the clause of exception as far as the hadith of Abū Hurayrah from the Prophet ﷺ is concerned: "This World is accursed; what(ever) is in it is accursed, *save* for the remembrance of Allāh and what approximates it, and *save* for a man of knowledge and a learner."[203] Al-Tirmidhī has reported it, saying: Hadith *ḥasan gharīb*.[204]

It has been narrated from ʿUbādah b. al-Ṣāmit ؓ that he said: The *dunyā* is brought on the Day of Rising, and the Lord, Blessed and Exalted is He, will say: Take out all that is in it that belongs to Us and throw the rest of it in the Fire.

CHAPTER 10 (37)

EXPLANATION OF THIS WORLD AND THE METAPHORS COINED FOR IT

Allāh ﷻ said: *The metaphor of the life of the* dunyā *is that of water which We send down from the sky, and which then mingles with the plants of the earth to provide food for both people and animals. Then, when the earth is at its loveliest and takes on its fairest guise and its people think they have it under their control, Our command comes upon it by night or day and We reduce it to dried-out stubble, as though it had not been flourishing just the day before!* (10:24). He also said ﷻ: *Know that the life of the* dunyā *is merely a game and a diversion and ostentation and a cause of boasting among yourselves and trying to outdo one another in wealth and children: like the plant-growth after rain which delights the cultivators, but then it withers and you see it turning yellow, and then it becomes broken stubble* (57:19).[205] He further said ﷻ: *Do you not see that Allāh sends down water from the sky and threads it through the earth to emerge as springs and then by it brings forth crops of varying colors, which then wither and you see them turning yellow and then He makes them into broken stubble?* (39:20),[206] as well as other verses (of similar meaning). He furthermore said ﷻ: *Man has only to look at his food* (80:24).

Ibn Abī Khaythamah reported from al-Ḍaḥḥāk b. Sufyān that he said: The Messenger of Allāh ﷺ said to me: "O Ḍaḥḥāk, what is your food?" I said: "Meat and milk." He said: "Then it turns into what?" I said: "Into what you have verily come to know, Messenger of Allāh!" He said: "Allāh has indeed made what comes out of the son of Adam a metaphor for this World."[207]

Ubayy b. Kaʿb said: The Prophet ﷺ said: "The food of the son of Adam has been made a metaphor for this World. If he seasons and salts it, let him look at what it eventually becomes."[208]

Abū al-Walīd said: I asked (ʿAbdallāh) Ibn ʿUmar about the man who gets inside a wilderness and looks at what comes out of him. He said: "The angel comes to him and says: Look at what was melted thereby into what it became of it."

Our people of knowledge, Allāh's mercy be upon them, have said: There are nine wonders of eloquent expression in Allāh's metaphorical description of this World by the water sent down from the sky:

1) Just as water is not called down by a stratagem, so this World is not attained save by capture. Allāh ﷻ has said: *We have allocated their livelihood among them in the life of the* dunyā (43:31);[209]

2) Though rain does not come except by Decree, nevertheless it is called down by desire and supplication. In the same way, worldly provision (*rizq*) is sought from Allāh. Allāh ﷻ has said: [*B*]*ut ask Allāh for His bounty* (4:32);

3) If He brings down rain it benefits, although, if it exceeds the limit of need, it causes harm. In likewise fashion, the owner of wealth is in bliss if it stays within the boundary of sufficiency, whereas, if it is in excess, it places its owner in a state of exhausting hardship and gripping oppression;

4) If water is running it is pleasing, but when it stagnates, hoarded in a storing place, it undergoes a transformation. The same holds true of wealth: It is delightfully good and agreeable when its owner makes it circulate in its right channels, but as soon as he withdraws it (turning it into a concealed form of accumulation), it becomes bad for him and is swallowed up in a void. Allāh ﷻ has said: *Those who are tight-fisted with the bounty Allāh has given them should not suppose that that is better for them. No indeed, it is worse for them! What they were tight-fisted with will be hung around their necks on the Day of Rising* (3:180);

5) Water that is pure is suitable for clothing and acts of worship, and water that is impure is unsuitable for acts of worship. Similarly, livelihood and obedience are both put upright by wealth that is licit, which is also safe from people's claims over it. As for wealth that is illicit, if ...[210] you trace it back (to the one entitled thereto), it lays bare its defectiveness, and if you cause him to famish, it eliminates

its reverential inviolability (as a lawful asset one blissfully enjoys and disposes of);

6) Whenever plants arise out of water and spread around, trees sprout forth, fruits ripen, cascading in different forms and shapes on the onlookers, the farmer has no assurance that a calamity is not going to strike his cultivated land without any apparent cause, nor that its state is not going to be turned upside down by something which had never been brought into any antecedent reckoning. When, identically to it, wealth grows in its owner's hands, he employs it proficiently in the various arts of investment, satisfying thereby the whole spectrum of his pleasures, and an abundance of wives and children is bestowed upon him (by virtue thereof). He basks accordingly in the perceived cloudless serenity of his states, elevation of his rank, high-valued nature of his resources, mutual proximity of his assets, radiant blossoming of the meadows in his plot, alternation of the branches of the surroundings' social affability and his intimate joy, when, lo! destruction seizes the houses, loss of the beloved befalls him, the assets smile in the grasp of despoliation's hand, and he makes off with those assets he places his greatest hopes on, which he is in most need of, and which he is most pleased with and yearns for the most as they fill him with the most extensive delight. On this meaning al-Maghribī wrote: "We lost it[211] when it reached its perfection and exulted in sublimity[212] / Like that is the eclipse of the full moon when its cycle is completed."

7) His Statement ﷻ: [*B*]*ut then becomes dry chaff scattered by the winds* (18:44).[213] If such alteration mentioned therein is due to some calamity occasioning crop damage, then this verse and the one after it converge in conveying the same meaning. If, on the other hand, this is that variety of crop the grains of which put out germinal seeds with plentiful covering peel,[214] and then it becomes dry chaff scattered by the winds or an ephemeral entity that vanishes away, by which the earth manifests its generosity and intermittently gushes forth with, that would be a metaphor in His uniquely wonderful mode of expression, namely, the next such wonder of eloquence:

8) That if the slave takes from wealth the quantum that fulfils the need of his livelihood, consuming the rest in appetites of the self, such wealth is vanished into non-existence in respect of this World, it is dry chaff, and its owner, because of it, becomes blamed, his time turning into something reprehensible;

9) From the viewpoint of reminders, the crops of varying colors, which then

wither and you see them turning yellow and then He makes them into broken stubble, shed alerting light on the differing states a crop goes through from its creation to its growth and its eventual coming into man's hands, from its first formation, that is, until its demise. As a planted seed does not send out its crop except after a phase of desiccation, likewise a person's action is not good unless and until he coaches and tames his self, and removes[215] before he is reverted to the meanest age, i.e., the condition of weakness in one's vital forces, and debilitation of the organs. The Prophet ﷺ used to say: "O Allāh, I seek refuge in You from being reverted to the lowest phase in a man's lifespan."[216] As for the metaphor of the Prophet ﷺ to the effect that this World educates man, its meaning is manifest. One of the virtuous people, in turn, likened this World to the corpse which (even) dogs refrain from, saying:

> It is nothing but a converted corpse[217]
> over which are dogs whose concern is to entice it
> If you avoid it you are at peace with those suited thereto
> But if you allure it and win it over, the dogs will dispute with you over it, and attempt to wrest it from you
> Blessedness to the self fond of the depth of its home[218]
> the doors whereof are shut and the curtains of which are lowered.

The aforesaid verses were penned by al-Shāfiʿī, Allāh have Mercy on him.[219]

CHAPTER 11 (38)

THE WORLD AS A PRISON OF THE BELIEVER AND GARDEN FOR THE DISBELIEVER

Muslim has reported on the authority of Abū Hurayrah that he said: The Messenger of Allāh ﷺ said: "This World is the prison of the *mu'min* and the Garden of the *kāfir*."[220]

This World is a prison because in it the *mu'min* is fettered by the restrictions imposed by divinely legislated obligations.[221] He thus has no freedom of movement or stillness save insofar as the law makes him room for that, thereby loosening the shackle on him and enabling him to carry out an action or abstain from it, as the case might be, with all the varieties of affliction and ordeal[222] entailed for him by the above. In addition, in this prison he experiences the utmost degree of fear and alarming anxiety, since he does not know which action is going to seal off his earthly life. The *kāfir*, by contrast, is set loose from such obligations, is safe from those sources of alarm, devotes himself to his pleasures, persistently pursues his appetites with eager earnestness, and is deceived by the (apparent) assistance lent him by the passing of the days, eating and enjoying himself in the manner of beasts, until he soon awakens from these dreams and ends up in the unwanted prison.

A story: Sahl al-Ṣuʿlūkī, the Ḥanafī jurisprudent from the region of Khurāsān, used to conjoin leadership in matters of *dīn* and *dunyā* alike. One day, while with his escort of attendants, he was in the heater of a public bath, a Jew in tatters, exiting his hostel slowly, came forward to him and said: "Are you not those narrating from your Prophet ﷺ that this World is the prison of the believer and the Garden of the unbeliever who covers up the truth? I, for that matter, am a *kāfir* slave, yet you see what my condition is, whereas you are a *mu'min* and your condition is in front of your eyes." Sahl al-Ṣuʿlūkī intuitively replied to him at once: "If you end up tomorrow in Allāh's punishment, this one is your Garden, and if I end up in Allāh's bliss and in His satisfaction, this one is my prison." People were astonished by his sharp understanding and expressive proficiency. This narration is very authentic.

As for the *ḥasan* hadith (on this issue), the following has been related: "This World is the *mu'min's* prison and barren land. When he departs from this World he departs from the prison and the arid soil."[223] Abū Bakr b. al-ʿArabī mentioned it in his book *Sirāj al-murīdīn*.[224]

CHAPTER 12 (39)

DESIRING THE OTHER WORLD AND FOREGOING THE ADORNMENTS OF THIS WORLD

Al-Tirmidhī reported on the authority of (ʿAbdallāh) b. Masʿūd ﷺ that he said: The Messenger of Allāh ﷺ said: "Be ashamed vis-à-vis Allāh to the degree that is proper." We said: "Messenger of Allāh, we do display modest shame vis-à-vis Allāh, praise be to Allāh." He said: "That is not it. The true measure of shame vis-à-vis Allāh is to guard the head and the real understanding it encompasses, to guard the stomach and what it contains, and to remember death and testing affliction. Whoever desires the Other World should forgo the adornment of this World. The one who does so has verily showed the true measure of shame vis-à-vis Allāh."[225] He commented: Hadith *gharīb*.

Allāh ﷻ has said, elucidating the meaning of the adornment of this World: *We made everything on the earth adornment for it* (18:7). He also said ﷻ: *Wealth and sons are the embellishment of the life of the* dunyā (18:45).[226] He further said: *To mankind the love of worldly appetites is painted in glowing colors: women and children* (3:14).[227]

A statement comparable thereto from the Sunnah is his saying ﷺ "This World is (like) sweet, succulently tender and fresh greenery, and Allāh has appointed you as vicegerents in it in order to see how you act"[228]; as well as his saying ﷺ "What I fear most for you is the flower of this World which Allāh issues forth for you." They asked: "And what is the flower of this World?" He replied: "The delightful produce of the earth."[229] Muslm reported the aforesaid pair of statements from the narration of Abū Saʿīd al-Khudrī.

The meaning is that this World is something deemed pleasant in the tasting thereof, which delights with its guise the way the likeable date pleases the one looking at it. Yet Allāh has tested His slaves by it to see which of them is best in action, i.e., which of them does away with it[230] and renounces it the most, in conformity with what we have mentioned hereabove. The slave has no route to some of what Allāh has created as adornment save by His power over it.[231]

Because of that, ʿUmar ؓ used to say, based on what al-Bukhārī has reported: "O Allāh, we are incapable of rejoicing in what You have adorned for us. O Allāh, I ask you to enable me to spend it in what is entitled thereto as its due." He thus supplicated Allāh to help him spend it appropriately.

In the same semantic vein is his statement ﷺ: "Whoever takes it spontaneously is blessed in it, and whoever appropriates it by deliberate self-management[232] is like the one who eats without being satiated."[233] The latter is the one who collects an abundant supply of this World, and who is not contented with the portion thereof that falls to his lot, since his concern is to gather it (to the maximum degree possible). That is the upshot of a lack of understanding about Allāh and His Messenger. In his state, faith is put to the test and safety is predominantly missing, as it has been previously remarked. Victory is for the one who submits (to the will of Allāh) and is granted a sufficient modicum of sustenance, Allāh placing in his heart contentment with what He has provided him with.[234]

CHAPTER 13 (40)

THE PROPHET'S STATEMENT: "WHOEVER LOATHES MY SUNNAH IS NOT OF ME"

Al-Bukhārī and Muslim reported from Anas (b. Mālik), the wording being that of al-Bukhārī, that he said: Three groups of people came to the apartments of the wives of the Prophet ﷺ asking questions about the Prophet's worship. When they were informed about how it was, it was as if they were disputing it. They said: "Where do we stand in comparison with the Prophet ﷺ! He has been forgiven all his earlier errors and any later ones." One of them said: "As for me, I spend the whole night in prayer every day." Another one said: "I fast all days without ever leaving one day for the diurnal partaking of food." A third one said: "And I stay away from women without ever getting married." The Messenger of Allāh ﷺ came and said: "Are you the ones who said this and that? By Allāh, I certainly fear Allāh the most and circumspectly guard myself by what is pleasing to Him more than any of you. Yet I fast and do not fast, I pray and take a break from prayer, and I marry women. Whoever loathes my Sunnah is not of me."[235]

Muslim has reported on the authority of Saᶜd b. Abī Waqqāṣ that he said: ᶜUthmān b. Maẓᶜūn[236] wanted to remain celibate, so the Prophet ﷺ forbade him that. Had it been permissible for him [Saᶜd commented], we would have followed his example and curbed our desire for women.

Al-Tirmidhī al-Ḥakīm, Abū ᶜAbdallāh, reported in his book *Nawādir al-uṣūl*, on the authority of Saᶜīd b. al-Musayyib, that he said: ᶜUthmān b. Maẓᶜūn came to the Messenger of Allāh ﷺ and said: "O Messenger of Allāh, the self's whispering talk has overcome me, so I deemed it right not to embark on any new step until I mentioned that to you." The Messenger of Allāh ﷺ asked him: "And what does your self say to you, ʿUthmān?" He said: "My self tells me to adopt celibacy." He said: "Take it easy, ʿUthmān. The renunciation[237] of my ummah is fasting." He said: "Messenger of Allāh, my self tells me to lead a monastic life on a mountain summit." He said: "Take it easy, ʿUthmān. The monasticism of my ummah is to sit in the mosques and wait for the prayer." He said: "Messenger of Allāh, my self instructs me by words to roam around in the earth." He said: "Take it easy, ʿUthmān. The roaming around of my ummah is to conduct military raids in the path of Allāh, and to perform the hajj and the umrah." He said: "Messenger of Allāh, my self tells me to give up my entire wealth." He said: "Take it easy, ʿUthmān. Your giving out *ṣadaqah* every day, holding yourself and your family back (from full self-gratification), having mercy on the destitute and on the orphan, and feeding the latter, is better than that (which you have mentioned)." He said: "Messenger of Allāh, my self says to me that I should divorce my wife Khawlah and flee." He said: "Take it easy, ʿUthmān. Migration in my ummah is to migrate away from what Allāh has prohibited, or to make *hijrah* to where I am during my lifetime, or to visit my grave after I die, even if any such member of my nation were to die leaving behind two or three or four wives." He said: "Messenger of Allāh, you have enjoined me not to divorce her, but in its conversation my self exhorts me not to cohabit with her." He said: "Take it easy, ʿUthmān. Whenever the Muslim man cohabits with his wife or one whom his right hand possesses, without any progeny resulting from such intercourse, he will have a valet serving him in the Garden; and if that very same intercourse begets a child, he will be for him, on the Day of Rising, a predecessor who precedes him in entering it and an intercessor for him if such child dies before him, or a light for him if he passes away after him." He said: "Messenger of Allāh, my self tells me not to touch perfume." He said: "Take it easy, ʿUthmān. [the angel] Jibrīl brought to me perfume from the Garden at constant intervals, and said: 'Do not forget to put it on every Friday.' ʿUthmān, do not loathe my Sunnah. Whoever loathes my Sunnah and renounces it, and then dies before seeking forgiveness for that, the angels will turn his face away from my pool[238] on the Day of Rising."[239]

It has become clear to you, brother, from what has been mentioned both in this chapter and in the antecedent ones, that renouncing the permissible things and forbidding the good kinds of provision is not part of *zuhd.*

Allāh ﷻ has said: *Say: 'Who has forbidden the fine clothing Allāh has produced for His slaves and the good kinds of provision?* (7:30).[240]

He also said ﷻ: *Messengers, eat of the good things and act rightly* (23:52).[241]

He further said ﷻ: *We sent them Messengers before you and gave them wives and children* (13:39).[242]

The verses conveying this meaning are aplenty.

If it were to be said: It has been narrated from Jābir (b. ʿAbdallāh) that he said: "My family desired meat, so I purchased some for them. On my way from buying it I chanced upon ʿUmar b. al-Khaṭṭāb ﷺ 'What is this, Jābir?' I informed him of the aforesaid, whereupon he commented: 'Does that mean that whenever one of you[243] desires something he puts it in his stomach? Are you[244] not afraid to be one of the people referred to in this verse: *You dissipated the good things you had in your worldly life?*'"(46:19).[245] the reply thereto would be as follows: This is a reprimand to him by ʿUmar for liberal self-expansion in this World and, through the purchase of meat, for departing from the crude nourishing basis of bread and water (only), as al-Tirmidhī has narrated from ʿUthmān (b. ʿAffān) in the aforementioned report. Natural dispositions deteriorate, and habit settles in on an ongoing basis, by busying oneself with the pursuit of the good kinds of provision that are lawful. When such a nature and such a habit lose such things, they succumb to the impulse of acquiring them by dubious means until they fall into the forbidden pure and simple, with a concomitant worsening of the self that constantly commands evil, such a jump being the predominant usual development of the aforesaid. Accordingly, ʿUmar grabbed the matter at its source, and protected him at its point of inception, the way the likes of ʿUmar are wont to do.

ʿAlī, ﷺ has indeed stated, when the *fālūdhaj* was brought to him: "I do not declare it to be prohibited. I dislike, though, to accustom my self to a habit it had not developed."

The judge Abū Bakr b. al-ʿArabī has said: What precisely defines this discourse for you, and establishes its guiding principle in a balanced way, is that the man of *zuhd* eats whatever he finds, whether pleasant or plain, without forcing himself to seek out and stick to the pleasant. The Prophet ﷺ used to eat his fill whenever he found it, and exercise patient restraint if he did not. He used to eat sweetmeats if he had the opportunity, and partake of honey if that happened for him. And he used to eat meat when that was made easy for him without habitually eating it or making that his customary practice. The livelihood of the Prophet ﷺ is well-known, and the usual way of the companions with food has been transmitted down to us.

As for the present times, when the unlawful has gained the ascendancy, and worldly vanities have spread corruption, salvation is hard. Allāh grants the gift of salvation, and helps attain it. He is the supporting protector and the guarding defender of the truthful admonisher.

It is unbefitting to leave out mention of the *mas'alah* taking the form of a complementary coda to this book, rather, understanding and learning it is indispensable.

What the people of knowledge have said about it encompasses what we have narrated to the effect that the Imam Abū ʿUmar b. ʿAbd al-Barr, may Allāh show mercy on him, said, upon being informed of the criticism levelled at him by a group of people from Shāṭibah about his eating the food of the political authorities and accepting their monetary rewards:

> Tell the one who mentions my eating
> from the food of the rulers:
> In this ignorance of yours
> you're in the position of the fools.

That is so since emulating the righteous models from among the companions, the followers, those firmly rooted in knowledge and the Muslim leaders of fatwa from the bygone generations, is in fact the fundament and essential prerequisite of the *dīn*.

Zayd b. Thābit, who was among those firmly rooted in knowledge, used to accept the monetary rewards of Muʿāwiyah and of his son Yazīd. And [ʿAbdallāh] Ibn ʿUmar, with all his scrupulousness and virtue, used to accept the gifts of his in-law al-Mukhtār b. Abī ʿUbaydillāh (*sic*), as well eating his food and taking his monetary rewards, despite the fact that al-Mukhtār (literally meaning: the choice one) was anything but choice.

ʿAbdallāh b. Masʿūd, who was filled with knowledge, replied as follows to a man who had asked him the following: "I have a neighbor transacting in usury and not refraining from the unlawful in his earnings, who invites me to partake of his food and whose invitation I accept. [Is it correct for me to do so?]." "Yes (ᶜAbdallāh b. Masᶜūd said), for you the felicitous swallowing of what agrees with your nature and for him the sin, so long as you do not positively identify the very thing partaken of as an unlawfully acquired wealth."[246]

As for ᶜUthmān b. ᶜAffān ﷺ; he said, when asked about the rewarding grants of the rulers: savory gazelle meat.

Al-Shaᶜbī, one of the foremost followers from among their men of knowledge, used to discipline[247] the sons of ᶜAbd al-Mālik b. Marwān, yet he would accept his grants and partake of his food.

Ibrāhīm al-Nakhaᶜī, the rest of the scholars of al-Kūfah, al-Ḥasan al-Baṣrī[248] (his *zuhd* and scrupulousness in the *dīn* notwithstanding), together with the remainder of the people of knowledge in al-Baṣrah, Abū Salamah b. ᶜAbd al-Rahmān and Abān b. ᶜUthmān, as well as all the seven *fuqahā'* of al-Madīnah,[249] with the exception of Saᶜīd b. al-Musayyib, used to accept the grants of the political rulers.

Ibn Shihāb (al-Zuhrī) used to accept them, too, and dispose of them.[250] They represented the bulk of his earnings. Likewise with Abū al-Zinād. And Mālik, Abū Yūsuf, al-Shāfiᶜī and other jurists from al-ᶜIrāq and al-Ḥijāz, also used to accept the allowances of the sultans and the amirs.

Regardless of his scrupulousness and virtue, Sufyān al-Thawrī used to mention that the grants of the political authority were dearer to him than the gifts of the friendly brothers (in the *dīn*), since the fraternal coreligionists, unlike the political ruler, would accompany their munificence by demands for gratitude (*yamunnūn*).[251]

Several such sayings, which people have strewn together in full chapters of books, have originated with our virtuous men of knowledge.

Aḥmad b. Khālid, the jurist and savant of al-Andalus, authored a book which he devoted to his own situation, filling it with the various derogatory attacks against him by his fellow townsmen arising out of his acceptance of ᶜAbd al-Raḥmān al-Nāṣir's grants. ᶜAbd al-Raḥmān al-Nāṣir, in fact, had him move to the city center of Cordova, lodged him in one of the houses attached to its primary mosque,[252] drew him close to him, and maintained him with basic food and condiments, as well as with security personnel. Aḥmad b. Khālid and his likes had monetary shares apportioned to them in the public treasury (*bayt al-*

māl), and the aforementioned sultan was personally responsible for ensuring that such allotments would not get mixed up.

As ᶜAbdallāh b. Masᶜūd said, for you the felicitous swallowing of what agrees with your nature and for him the sin, so long as you do not positively identify the very thing partaken of as an unlawfully acquired wealth. This is something the veracity of which has been established by the consensus of opinions among the prominent people of knowledge: Whenever one knows that a specific thing is illicit, having been appropriated in an unlawful manner, such as a particular unit of bread or some other foodstuff or an individualized livestock or some other demarcated thing that has been usurped, stolen or seized by plainly unjust means beyond any obfuscating doubt, no one differs concerning the fact that it is forbidden, that the testimony of the one partaking of it is rejected since he is not an admissible witness of integrity, and that receiving or acquiring ownership over such a thing is similarly proscribed. I know of no follower who scrupulously stayed away from the allowances of the political rulers save for the dual exception of Saᶜīd b. al-Musayyib in al-Madīnah and of Muḥammad b. Sīrīn in al-Baṣrah, both of whom have been elevated to the rank of paradigms of utmost scrupulousness. One counts, among those who followed in their footsteps, Aḥmad b. Ḥanbal and the people of *zuhd*, scrupulousness in the *dīn* and asceticism, may Allāh have mercy on all of them.

To exercise *zuhd* in this World is one of the most meritorious virtues. Yet it is not permissible for one whom Allāh ﷻ has granted success to, and who has done without in this World, to declare what Allāh ﷻ has permitted of it to be prohibited. How astonishingly odd are the people of this time who decry and find fault with the dubious things while declaring the forbidden things to be lawful. Their likeness in my view is that of the people who asked ᶜAbdallāh b. ᶜUmar ﷺ about the person wearing the *iḥrām* who kills the locusts and lice, whereupon he said to such questioners: "From where are you?" They replied: "From the inhabitants of al-Kūfah." He commented: "You ask about this and yet you are the ones who killed al-Ḥusayn b. ᶜAlī ﷺ!"

(ᶜAbdallāh) Ibn ᶜUmar narrated from the Prophet ﷺ that he said: "Take whatever comes to you without you asking for it, and make it your own."[253] This hadith has also been narrated from Ibn ᶜUmar from the Prophet ﷺ: "Eat whatever comes to you without you asking for it, and make it your own."

Abū Saᶜīd al-Khudrī and Jābir b. ᶜAbdallāh have both narrated from the Prophet ﷺ not literally but in terms of its meaning: "It is but a provision which Allāh has bestowed upon you," in the hadith of one of the two of them. The wording of some of the narrators thereof is: "The provision of Allāh is not returned to Him."

The aforementioned, in its full compass, is built on what they had unanimous consensus about, and it is the truth.[254]

I said: This is the end of Abū ᶜUmar (b. ᶜAbd al-Barr)'s speech, may Allāh shower him with Mercy.

In his book *al-Maᶜālim*,[255] a commentary on Abū Dāwud's *Sunan*, al-Khattābī, Abū Sulaymān, alluded to the aforementioned in the course of his clarifying speech about his statement ﷺ: "The lawful is clear and the prohibited is clear,"[256] where he said at the end of his elucidation of this hadith: Within the folds of this discourse one tackles the case of dealing with someone whose wealth is tainted by some obfuscating doubt about its lawfulness or which is mixed with usury. The preferred view is to keep away from dealing with such a person in favor of dealing with other than him. There is no forbidden action on our part, however, if we deal with him so long as no certainty prevails that the very same object of the interaction is unlawful and that, accordingly, the context of its public production is unlawful.

The Messenger of Allāh ﷺ gave his armor in pledge to a Jew in exchange for measures[257] of barley which he took into his possession for the daily nourishment of his family.[258] It is known that they (the Jews) charge usury in their trading transactions and view the price fetched by intoxicants as lawful. It follows from the above that it is disallowed for one who believes in Allāh and the Last Day to prohibit what Allāh has made permissible without knowledge and discerning insight. The following statement by Hishām b. ᶜAmmār is linked to what has been stated hereabove, confirming it emphatically and entrenching it more decisively:

I came to Mālik b. Anas in al-Madīnah while he was sitting at the center of a mattress he was sunk in. Some eunuchs, wielding fly swatters whereby they protected him from flies, were standing over his shoulders. I said: "O Abā ᶜAbdallāh,[259] narrate to me some Prophetic sayings." Mālik said (to his attendants): "Seat him comfortably."[260] Hishām said: "I was thus carried to a place in front of him, so I turned my attention to him, saying: 'O Abā ᶜAbdallāh, by the One whom you ask to show mercy to your abased standing in front of Him, should you not show mercy to my abased standing in front of you?' He (Mālik) said: 'Take him back (where he was).'" He then narrated to me nineteen Prophetic sayings ﷺ.

The Imām Abū Ḥāmid (al-Ghazālī), in the section about the cure of glorious feats and commendable deeds from his book *Minhāj al-ᶜābidīn*,[261] mentioned the following:

"If it were to be said: What does one assert concerning the acceptance of the rulers' grants in this epoch? The reply to such question would be as follows: 'Know that the views of the people of knowledge have differed in this regard. One group claimed that it is permissible to take whatever is not known for certain to be an unlawful property. Another group alleged that one is not allowed to take anything that is not known for sure to be a lawful asset, given that the forbidden is what is dominant among rulers in this age, and that the permissible in their possession is a precious rarity or non-existent. Yet a third group affirmed that the gifts of the rulers are licit for both the poor and the rich, provided their prohibited nature is not an established fact, and that any responsibility attaches to the grantor only.[262] They say in support of their opinion: Because the Prophet ﷺ accepted the gift of the king of Alexandria, and borrowed from the Jew despite the statement of Allāh ﷻ: *They are people who listen to lies* (5:42). A number (of companions), *inter alia* Abū Hurayrah, (ᶜAbdallāh) Ibn ᶜAbbās and (ᶜAbdallāh) Ibn ᶜUmar, lived long enough to witness the age of the unjust rulers. As for a fourth group, they averred that none of their properties was permissible for either the poor or the rich, since they became opulent (precisely) through injustice, and their prevalent condition was one of ill-gotten gains and ownership of the unlawful, whence the ineluctable obligation of steering clear (of their wealth).

A further group contended that whatever is not known to be surely unlawful is permissible for the poor but not the rich man, save insofar as the poor man knows that the very property given as a grant has been usurped, in which event he is only entitled to take it for the purpose of returning it to its rightful owner (it has been usurped from). In such matter, no tight restriction stands in the way of the poor man who entertains no doubt about its lawfulness. He can take such property, even if it falls part of the war-booty acquired without actual fighting (*al-fay'*), the land tax (*al-kharāj*) or what is levied on the lands whose proprietors embrace Islam at a time when they enjoy the ownership thereof (*al-ᶜushr* or *al-ᶜashīr*).[263] The poor man has in fact an entrenched right to it (in any case). The same is true of the qualified devotees of knowledge. ᶜAlī b. Abī Ṭālib ﷺ said: 'Whoever embraces Islam in a famished state and reads the Qur'ān has a lawful entitlement to an annual share of 100 silver coins from the Muslims' public treasury.'[264] Mālik b. Dīnār said: 'If he does not take receipt of it in this World he will do so in the Next World.' Given the aforementioned, the poor man and the scholar merely take exactly what is due to them (in the first place).

They have also said: If the wealth in question is mixed with usurped one, with no possibility of differentiation between the two, or it is the very fruit of usurpation that can be returned neither to its rightful owner (it has been usurped from) nor to his offspring, the ruler cannot escape from disposing of it personally as his sole option. It is not for Allāh to command him to give it in *ṣadaqah* to the indigent man, when such destitute person is forbidden from taking receipt thereof, or to command him to grant the poor man permission to accept it, when such property is unlawful for the poor man.

In short, therefore, the poor man is extended the right to accept any such property except the very usurped asset that is unlawful, which he cannot receive into his possession.'"

ᶜAbdallāh Muḥammad al-Mālikī stated in his work *Aḥkām al-Qur'ān*:

"With regard to taking the unjust rulers' provisions, know that they fall under three categories:

1) All the property in their hands has been acquired in accordance with the shariah. In such case, receiving any of it is permissible. The companions and the followers received wealth at the hands of al-Ḥajjāj and others;

2) It is a blend of the lawful and the ill-gotten,[265] as is the wealth of today's rulers. The scrupulous approach is not to take any such provision. It is however permitted to the needy person to receive it, since in his hands it is pure and unadulterated.[266] Masrūq said: In this category falls the wholesome and lawful wealth which a man entrusts to another as his agent, whereupon a thief comes, and then gives out some of it in *ṣadaqah*, the stolen property in itself not being known in this scenario (in which instance the needy man can lawfully

take receipt of such *ṣadaqah*). In like manner, if he were to sell or purchase it, the contract of sale regarding such article would be legally valid and binding. Scrupulousness, however, lies in avoiding association with such (mixed) wealth, since wealth acquires its status of unlawfulness in its generality, not on the basis of its single constituent units;

3) What(ever) is in their hands is ill-gotten and unlawful. It is impermissible to take any of it. Or what is in their hands is usurped wealth the rightful owner whereof is unknown and which no claimant is laying a claim to, as is the case with what is found in the possession of thieves and robbers. It is stored in the public treasury, and as much time as possible is granted for its (rightful) claimant to come forward. If, however, its owner is unknown and remains so after the lapse of a reasonable time, the political leader disposes of it in utilities aimed at benefiting the well-being of the Muslims."

I said: This is the statement of the people of knowledge that I came across in this *mas'alah*. All of them concur as to the impermissibility of acquiring or receiving individually demarcated property of undiluted unlawfulness. Concerning whatever belongs to a different category, forgoing it represents the scrupulous option.

We have laid out this meaning before in sufficient detail, in the twelfth chapter (of this overall work). Herein we cast additional light on this subject, the proper place and time for mention whereof being herein. Praise for that is Allāh's. There is no Lord and no worshipped one but He, Exalted and Glorified above any association is He. To Allāh belong the praise and the gracious kindness. Thankfulness is owed to Him for the blessings that He beneficently willed and conferred, and His is the merit for whatever is understood and embraced by knowledge. Allāh has sent blessings and peace upon Muḥammad, his slave and Prophet, and He has lauded and extolled (him).

This book was completed by the praise and assistance of Allāh. Praise be to Allāh, the Lord of all the worlds. Allāh, send blessings on Muḥammad whenever the people of remembrance mention him, and whenever the neglectful neglect to remember him.

APPENDIX ONE

THE *ABDĀL*

"The *abdāl* in this ummah are thirty men. Their hearts are on the heart of Ibrāhīm, the intimate friend of the Merciful. Whenever one such man passes away, Allāh puts another man in his place, as his substitute." This hadith has been narrated on the authority of ʿUbādah b. al-Ṣāmit. Aḥmad reported it in his *Musnad*. Al-Haythamī said that the transmitters in the chain of this hadith were transmitters of authentic narrations, save for ʿAbd al-Wāḥid b. Qays on whom the views of evaluators of transmitters differed [al-ʿIjlī and Abū Zurʿah pronounced him to be reliable, whereas others declared him weak].

In *al-Jāmiʿ al-ṣaghīr*, al-Suyūṭī referred to it with the mark symbolizing an authentic (*ṣaḥīḥ*) hadith. In the famous commentary on such collection of narrations, *Fayḍ al-qadīr*, the great Egyptian scholar and Sufi al-Munāwī said that the word *abdāl* was the plural of *badal*. Allāh the Exalted singled them out by bestowing on them certain qualities specific to them. For example, they lean in their states on Allāh without stirring motion. Another peculiar characteristic is their refinement and good character traits. It has been mentioned that they have been given the name *abdāl* because, when they are absent, spiritual forms standing in their places substitute for them. A path to Allāh the Exalted has been opened to them which accords to the path of Ibrāhīm ﷺ. Another recension says: "Their hearts are upon the heart of a single man." Al-Ḥakīm (al-Tirmidhī) said the only reason for that was that their hearts have become oblivious of everything but Him, so they became connected to Him with a single, unified connection. They have thus become as if they are one and the same heart.

He (Ibn al-ʿArabī) said in *al-Futūḥāt* that his statement here "on the heart of Ibrāhīm," the one in another narration on the heart of Adam 🕊, and his saying concerning others on the heart of one of the great human beings or angels, all those utterances bear the meaning that they move around in the fields of Divine gnosis by the heart of such creature (man or angel). That is so the Divine sciences come upon the hearts of all loci. Every knowledge, therefore, that descends on the heart of such a majestic angel or human likewise descends on the hearts of such men who are set on his heart. One possibly says in Arabic: So-and-so is upon the foot of so-an-so. Its connotation is what has been mentioned by the Sufi litterateur al-Qayṣarī al-Rūmī as having been said by the gnostic Ibn al-ʿArabī: 'He said "on the heart of Ibrāhīm" 🕊, because sainthood or *wilāyah* is absolute or restricted. The absolute one is the complete sainthood incorporating all the partial dimensions of sainthood, one by one and embracing all the single types thereof without exception. The restricted one is made up of those single components of sainthood. The manifestation of both the partial and the complete sainthood is something that is sought after and required. All the varieties of sainthood of the prophets have manifested themselves in this nation by inheritance from them. That is why in this narration he said here "on the heart of Ibrāhīm" 🕊, and in another hadith "on the heart of Mūsā" 🕊, or on the heart of so-and-so or on that of our Prophet Muḥammad 🕊, the possessor of the complete sainthood, as his is the perfected circle of full *wilāyah*. That is so because the inward dimension of that perfected prophethood is the complete and absolute sainthood. Since the sainthood of every prophet has its manifestation in this nation, one of the graces of the prophets is to have in this nation those who are upon the heart of one of the prophets.'

As for the last sentence of the hadith, "[w]henever one such man passes away, Allāh puts another man in his place, as his substitute," it is for that they have been named *abdāl*, meaning substitutes. Another possible interpretation of that name is that they replaced their evil character traits and disciplined themselves by training their selves until the virtuous aspects of their character became the decoration of their actions.

The outward indication of the speeches of the experts of *ḥaqīqah* is that the ranks of those thirty men vary. The gnostic (Abū al-ʿAbbās) al-Mursī said: 'I roamed around the *malakūt* and I saw Abū Madyan (al-Ghawth) clinging to the leg of the Throne. He was a fair-complexioned blue-eyed man. I said to him: What are your sciences and what is your station? He said: My sciences are seventy-one, and my station is that of the fourth of the caliphs (of the inner realm), and the head of the seven *abdāl*. I said to him then: al-Shādhilī has stated that that is an ocean that cannot be encompassed.' The gnostic (Abū al-ᶜAbbās) al-Mursī also said: 'I was sitting in front of my teacher al-Shādhilī when a group of people came to visit him. He (al-Shādhilī) said: Those are *abdāl*. I cast a look with my inner eye without perceiving them to be *abdāl*, so I plunged into a state of confusion. Then the Shaykh (al-Shādhilī) said: The one whose evil actions are turned into good actions as a substitute for the former, he is a *badal*. I thus understood that that was the first degree of *badaliyyah* or the state of being a *badal*.

Ibn ᶜAsākir (the great *ḥafiẓ* who *inter alia* authored the encyclopaedic *Tārīkh madīnat Dimashq*, or *The history of Damascus*) reported that Ibn al-Muthannā asked Aḥmad ibn Ḥanbal: What do you say about (the great Sufi) Bishr al-Ḥāfi ibn al-Ḥārith? He replied: 'The fourth-ranked of seven *abdāl*.'

There are of course several other prophetic narrations about the *abdāl*, five of which are enumerated in the said work by al-Suyūṭī and elucidated by the commentators thereon such as ᶜAbd al-Ra'ūf al-Munāwī. In addition, the various implications of the term have been expatiated upon in general Sufi texts, and in treatises devoted to Sufi terminology particularly or the technical lexicon of Islamic sciences generally, such as al-Jurjānī's *al-Taᶜrīfāt*, al-Munāwī's own corrigendum and compendium to the selfsame opus, as well as the Indian scholar al-Tahānawī's *Kashshāf muṣṭalaḥāt al-funūn*. These naturally cover the many accounts and anecdotes concerning the lives, states, characteristics, sayings, and deeds of famous *abdāl* renowned as part of such an elite group of His friends.

APPENDIX TWO

BIOGRAPHICAL NOTATIONS

The following are brief biographical notations of the persons cited in this text. Names are alphabetized as they appear in the text, disregarding diacritical marks and the Arabic definite article *al*.

ABĀN B. ʿUTHMĀN

Abān b. ʿUthmān b. ʿAffān al-Umawī al-Qurashī, Abū Saʿīd or Abū ʿAbdallāh (d. 105 AH). He was a trustworthy Madīnan follower and the caliph's son; he transmitted narrations from his father, Zayd b. Thābit, and Usāmah b. Zayd. Abū al-Zinād and al-Zuhrī were among those who took hadith from him. He was a reliable transmitter, with a solid understanding of the *fiqh* of hadith; Yaḥyā al-Qaṭṭān counted him as one of the seven *fuqahā'* of al-Madīnah, the city where he was born and died. He was struck with some deafness and leprosy, and one year prior to his death (during the rule of Yazīd b. ʿAbd al-Malik), he became semi-paralyzed, so he used to be carried to the mosque on a litter. He was the first to write on the subject of the Prophet's biography and the Prophet's military expeditions ﷺ, committing his contribution thereto to a written memorial. He handed his writing thereon to Sulaymān b. ʿAbd al-Malik in the course of his hajj in the year 82 AH, but in Sulaymān's care it was destroyed. What he wrote included jesting anecdotes, some of which were quoted by Abū al-Faraj al-Aṣbahānī, the author of *al-Aghānī*. He participated in the Battle of the Camel on ʿĀ'ishah's side and was given prominent influence by the Umayyads, a circumstance inclusive of his appointment as governor of al-Madīnah between 72 and 83 AH Mālik b. Anas is reported as saying that Abān knew some of his father's judgments and was the teacher of ʿAbdallāh, Abū Bakr's son. Aḥmad b. Ḥanbal denied that he directly heard any hadith from his father, yet his hadith transmission in Muslim's *Ṣaḥīḥ* explicitly affirms such firsthand reception of narrations from his father.

ʿABD AL-MALIK B. MARWĀN

ʿAbd al-Malik b. Marwān b. al-Ḥakam al-Umawī al-Qurashī (26–86 AH), one of the mightiest and cleverest caliphs, was a *faqīh*, devout worshipper, and pious ascetic of vast knowledge; he grew up in al-Madīnah.

ʿABD AL-RAḤMĀN AL-NĀṢIR

ʿAbd al-Raḥmān b. Muḥammad al-Nāṣir al-Marwānī al-Umawī, Abū al-Muṭarrif (288–350 AH). He was the first to take the designation of *khalīfah* (in his own right, rather than the title amir) among the Umayyad rulers in al-Andalus; he was a descendant of ʿAbd al-Raḥmān al-Dākhil (the first such ruler, i.e., the one who entered). He had in fact realized the weakness of al-Muqtadir al-ʿAbbāsī in ʿIrāq. His self-designation "al-Nāṣir li Dīn Allāh" (the Supporter of Allāh's Dīn) was appropriated by his successors. He was born and died in Cordova, and grew up as an orphan; he lost his father at the age of twenty-one and was brought up by his grandfather. His uncles, on account of his grandfather's special affection for him, were the first to swear allegiance to him. He was judicious, clever, full of praiseworthy virtues, a great peacemaker, and strongly ambitious as well. He devoted his energies to military conquests, urban development, and the erection of monuments. He built the city of al-Zahrā'. A famous historian called him the most majestic Umayyad ruler in Islamic Spain.

ʿABD AL-RAZZĀQ

ʿAbd al-Razzāq b. Hammām b. Nāfiʿ al-Ḥimyarī (by *walā'*), Abū Bakr al-Ṣanʿānī (a noun of ascription to the largest Yemeni city), (126-211 AH)He was a master of hadith transmission, used by all the authors of *al-Sittah*, about whom Aḥmad b. Ḥanbal said he had seen no one better than him in hadith. He transmitted *inter alia* from Mālik, al-Awzāʿī, and the two Sufyāns, al-Thawrī and Ibn ʿUyaynah, the latter being one of his *shuyūkh*, who in turn transmitted from ʿAbd al-Razzāq. Maʿmar said he was worthy of people beating the livers of the camels to travel to him and drink from his knowledge.

ᶜABDALLĀH MUḤAMMAD AL-MĀLIKĪ

As stated in *Aḥkām al-Qur'ān*: It might be a reference to Abū ᶜAbdallāh Muḥammad b. ᶜAbdallāh b. Abī Zamanayn al-Ilbīrī al-Andalusī (d. 399 AH), author of *al-Muntakhab fi al-aḥkām*, or to a contemporary of al-Qurṭubī, Abū ᶜAbdallāh Muḥammad b. ᶜĪsā b. Muḥammad al-Azdī, known as Ibn al-Munāṣif (d. 620 AH seven years before the writer hereof), who penned *al-Aḥkām wa al-shurūṭ*, and Allāh knows best.

ᶜABDALLĀH B. NUMAYR

ᶜAbdallāh b. Numayr al-Hamdānī al-Khārifī al-Kūfī, Abū Hishām (115–199 AH). He transmitted, among others, from al-Aᶜmash, Hishām b. ᶜUrwah, al-Awzāᶜī and Sufyān al-Thawrī. In the list of those who transmitted from him we find, together with his son Muḥammad, himself a great *muḥaddith*, Abū Bakr and ᶜUthmān, the two sons of the prestigious *muḥaddith* Abū Shaybah. Sufyān al-Thawrī, Yaḥyā b. Maᶜīn, Abū Ḥātim, Ibn Ḥibbān, al-ᶜIjlī, and Ibn Saᶜd unanimously eulogized him for his character, his *dīn*, and his hadith transmission.

ᶜABDALLĀH B. SHADDĀD

ᶜAbdallāh b. Shaddād b. al-Hād al-Laythī al-Madanī, Abū al-Walīd (d. 82 AH). He was used by all the compilers of *al-Sittah* and transmitted from most of the leading companions. His mother was the sister of Asmā', one of the reliable vanguards of knowledge and right action from the generation of the followers. The stronger view is that he was not killed (in the year 81 AH), but that the horses he and Ibn Abī Laylā were riding plunged themselves into water, and they could no longer be found.

ᶜABDALLĀH B. AL-ZUBAYR

ᶜAbdallāh b. al-Zubayr (1–73 AH). He was the full brother of ᶜUrwah b. al-Zubayr b. al-ᶜAwwām. His *kunyā* was Abū Bakr. He was Quraysh's horseman during his lifetime, and the first to be born in al-Madīnah after the hijrah. He took part in the conquest of northeast Africa under the caliphate of ᶜUthmān. He was sworn in as caliph in the year 64 AH, in the aftermath of Yazīd's death; he ruled over Egypt, the Ḥijāz, the Yemen, Khurāsān, the ᶜIrāq, and most of Greater Syria, making al-Madīnah the headquarters of his caliphate. Heavy battles occurred between him and the Umayyads, who eventually set al-Ḥajjāj out in pursuit in the time of ᶜAbd al-Malik b. Marwān. ᶜAbdallāh relocated to Makkah, whereas al-Ḥajjāj's troops encamped in al-Ṭā'if. Wars broke out between the two sides resulting in the dreadful assassination of ʿAbdallāh in Makkah after the bulk of his supporters deserted him. He fought heroically in his last battle, despite his very advanced age. His short-lived and tragic caliphate spanned seven years. He was the first to mint the circular silver coins. Such coins had writing on both sides, respectively: "Muḥammad al-Rasūlullāh" and "Allāh has commanded loyalty and justice." Thirty-three *aḥādīth* from him are recorded in the known collections. He was a reputed *khaṭīb*, drawing comparisons with Abū Bakr in that regard.

ABŪ AL-ASWAD AL-DUʿALĪ

Ẓālim b. ʿAmr b. Sufyān b. Jandal al- Duʿalī al-Kinānī, Abū al-Aswad (1 BH–69 AH). He was the founder of Arabic grammar. He conjoined *fiqh*, nobility, political leadership, chivalry, and promptness of speech. He is counted among the followers. ʿAlī b. Abī Ṭālib ﵁ traced for him a small part of the foundational principles of grammar on a piece of writing material, and Abū al-Aswad elaborated on it, meeting with the approval of people who took from it, though the author of *Ṣubḥ al-a'shā*, al-Qalqashandī, ascribed to him no more than the introduction of the vowelling and nunnation of words. He settled in al-Baṣrah during the caliphate of ʿUmar and became the governor thereof during the rule of ʿAlī ﵁. He took part on ʿAlī s side in the Battle of Ṣiffīn. When Muʿāwiyah ﵁ took over (al-Duʿalī having endured as governor until the assassination ofʿAlī in al-Baṣrah, where he died), he set out to meet Abū al-Aswad and honored him extensively. The majority view is that he was the first to place the diacritical marks on the letters of the *muṣḥaf* of the Qur'ān. He wrote poems of exquisite taste, collected in a *dīwān* that has been published.

ABŪ AL-ʿATĀHIYAH

Ismāʿīl b. al-Qāsim b. Suwayd al-ʿAynī al-'Anazī (from the tribe 'Anazah) by *walā'*, Abū Isḥāq known as Abū al-ʿAtāhiyah (130–211 AH) was a copious writer of innovative poetry, quick-witted, who used to compose 250 verses in one day, so much so that the gathering of his entire opus is an impossible task. He died in Baghdad.

ABŪ AYYŪB

Abū Ayyūb al-Anṣārī was a great companion; his name was Khālid b. Zayd (d. 50 or 51 AH). He took part in the *bayʿah* of al-ʿAqabah, in the battles of Badr, Uḥud, al-Khandaq, and the other ones in the time of the Prophet ﷺ. He passed away in Constantinople during the caliphate of Muʿāwiyah ؓ.

ABŪ BAKR B. AL-ʿARABĪ

Muḥammad b. ʿAbdallāh b. Muḥammad al-Maʿāfirī (from the tribe whose progenitor was Maʿāfir b. Yaʿfur, the lineage of whom is ultimately traced to Qaḥṭān) al-Ishbīlī (from his native town Sevilla), Abū Bakr (468–543 AH). He was a great Andalusian judge, *faqīh*, *muḥaddith*, *mujtahid*, historian, and more. For a period, he was the chief judge of Sevilla. He moved to Morocco and died in the close vicinity of Fez, where he is buried. The historian Ibn Bashkuwāl called him the seal of the *ʿulamā'* of al-Andalus, and the last of its imams and *ḥuffāẓ*. A small portion of his most distinguished historical-cum-theological and philosophical work, *al-ʿAwāṣim min al-qawāṣim*, has been translated into English under the title *Defence against disaster.*

ABŪ AL-ḤASAN AL-LAKHMĪ

He is ʿAlī b. Muḥammad al-Rabaʿī (d. 468 AH). He was from al-Qayrawān and settled in Sfax in present-day Tunisia. The Mālikī biographer Ibn Farḥūn said about his work *al-Tabṣirah*: A vast gloss on Saḥnūn's *al-Mudawwanah*. A manuscript thereof is found in the library of the Great Mosque in Tāzah, Morocco, under the catalogue numbers 213, 14, 15, 219.

ABŪ IDRĪS AL-KHAWLĀNĪ (ʿĀ'IDHULLĀH B. ʿABDALLĀH)

ʿĀ'idhullāh b. ʿAbdallāh b. ʿAmr, Abū Idrīs al-Khawlānī (8-80 AH), was a reliable hadith transmitter from the Followers, who was used as a narrator by all the compilers of the six canonical works on hadith. He transmitted from ʿUmar b. al-Khattāb, Abū al-Dardā', Muʿādh b. Jabal, Abū Dharr, Bilāl, ʿUbādah b. al-Sāmit, Abū Hurayrah, Abū Saʿīd al-Khudrī, and others. Al-Zuhrī was one of those who transmitted from him. He called him the relater and judge of Greater Syria during ʿAbd al-Malik's caliphate. He was described further as the most knowledgeable savant of Greater Syria after Abū al-Dardā'. In terms of encountering the choicest companions of the Messenger of Allāh ﷺ Abū Zurʿah said the best men of Greater Syria were Jubayr b. Nufayr and Abū Idrīs (al-Khawlānī).

ABŪ KABSHAH AL-ANMĀRĪ

Abū Kabshah al-Anmārī was a companion whose first name is the subject of discordant opinions among the genealogists, historians, and biographers. He settled in Greater Syria.

ABŪ KHALLĀD

Abū Khallād al-Ruʿaynī. In his biographical work on the companions, *al-Istīʿāb fī maʿrifat al-aṣḥāb*, the *ḥāfiẓ* of the Islamic West from Cordova, Ibn ʿAbd al-Barr said he could trace no first name or lineage for him.

ABŪ MASʿŪD

He is the companion al-Anṣārī al-Badrī. See the "Book of zakāt" in al-Bukhārī's *Ṣaḥīḥ*, "*Bāb ittaqū al-nāra wa law bi shiqqi tamratin, wa al-qalīli min al-ṣadaqah.*" In it we first find a narration from Sulaymān (al-Aʿmash) from Abū Wā'il from Abū Masʿūd ﵁ that he said: When the verse of *ṣadaqah* was revealed, we used to carry loads on our backs in exchange for a fee (exert ourselves in toiling effort which we bore patiently). A man came who gave out a large amount in *ṣadaqah*, and they said: 'A show-off!' Then another man came bringing only one *ṣāʿ* in *ṣadaqah*, and they commented: 'Allāh is not in need of only one such *ṣāʿ*.' Then the verse came down: *As for the people who find fault with those* mu'minun *who give* ṣadaqah *spontaneously* [Sūrah al-Tawbah, 9:80 in the Warsh *riwāyah*, 79 in others].

ABŪ MUṬĪʿ MAKḤŪL B. AL-FAḌL AL-NASAFĪ

Makḥūl b. al-Faḍl al-Nasafī, Abū Muṭīʿ (d. 318 AH) was a jurist who wrote a work on admonitions and counsels.

ABŪ QILĀBAH

ʿAbdallāh b. Zayd b. ʿAmr, Abū Qilābah al-Jarmī al-Baṣrī (d. ca. 107 AH) was one of the savants who transmitted from Zaynab bint Umm Salamah and a large number of companions and followers. Khālid al-Ḥadhdhā' and many others transmitted from him. He had his office in Greater Syria, narrated many *aḥādīth*, and was characterized by virtue, knowledge, judicial prowess, and according to Ibn Saʿd, al-ʿIjlī, and others, reliability in his transmission. He was a Baṣrīn follower, likewise utilized by all compilers of the six canonical collections.

ABŪ SALAMAH B. ᶜABD AL-RAHMĀN

Abū Salamah b. ᶜAbd al-Raḥmān b. ᶜAwf al-Zuhrī (d. 94 or 104 AH) the son of the noble companion; he was one of the great Madīnan jurists classified by some as the last of the seven *fuqahā'* of al-Madīnah. Al-Shaᶜbī narrated the following: Abū Salamah came to al-Kūfah and was walking between me and a third man when he was asked: "Who is the more knowledgeable of those still alive?" He refrained from answering and paused for a while, then replied: "A man between the two of us. Al-Zuhrī mentioned: Four I have found to be seas, Saᶜīd b. al-Musayyib, ᶜUrwah b. al-Zubayr, Abū Salamah b. ᶜAbd al-Raḥmān, and ᶜUbaydullāh b. ᶜAbdallāh b. Utbah b. Masᶜūd."

ABŪ SULAYMĀN AL-KHAṬṬĀBĪ

He is Ḥamad b. Muḥammad b. Ibrāhīm b. al-Khaṭṭāb al-Bustī (from Bust, a well-known town in the region of Sijastān, where he passed away), Abū Sulaymān (319–388 AH). He authored one of the most renowned and relied on commentaries of Abū Dāwud's *Sunan, Maᶜālim al-sunan.* He was a jurist as well, and devoted to poetry; he wrote good poems, some of which have been included by his friend al-Thaᶜālibī in his anthology *al-Yatīmah*, because of their artistic merit, not because of the existing bond of friendship. He was a descendant of Sayyidunā ᶜUmar's beloved brother, Zayd b. al-Khaṭṭāb (whence the noun of ascription he is famous by).

ABŪ ᶜUMAR B. ᶜABD AL-BARR

The *ḥāfiẓ* of the Islamic West, he is Yūsuf b. ᶜAbdallāh b. Muḥammad b. ᶜAbd al-Barr al-Namarī al-Qurṭubī al-Mālikī, Abū ᶜUmar, (368–463 AH). He was an encyclopaedia of *ᶜilm*, a historian, a man of literature, and a *faqīh* (his *al-Kāfī fī fiqh ahl al-Madīnah al-Mālikī* is one of the essential middle-sized juristic works following the Madīnan methodology). He travelled far and wide in eastern and western Spain, took up judicial appointments twice (including in present-day Portugal) and died in Shāṭibah, after having enriched the Islamic library with an assortment of splendid works in a wide range of multifarious fields, a significant segment of which have been published in numerous editions, e.g., *Jāmiᶜ bayān al-ᶜilm wa faḍlih*, his biographical masterpiece on the companions; *al-Istī'āb*, which we have quoted herein more than once; *Bahjat al-majālis wa uns al-mujālis*; and *Adab al-mujālasah wa faḍl al-lisān*, two works we intend translating in future, *inshallāh.* First and foremost are his various commentaries on Mālik's *al-Muwaṭṭa'*, especially *al-Istidhkār*; and the even more remarkable *al-Tamhīd*, based sequentially in the mode of a *musnad* of hadith, on the names of the (ultimate) narrators of the *aḥādīth* rather than the *fiqh*-inspired arrangement of chapters encountered in the text of *al-Muwaṭṭa'*. Of *al-Tamhīd*, the Andalusian leader of the Literalist school, Ibn Ḥazm, with all the notorious ferocious mordancy of his critical tongue, said he knew no other work on *fiqh* of hadith that was its equal, let alone one superior to it. Methodological discrepancies apart, the pair used to walk around, confabulate about things and extemporize poetry. Famous is the incident when during a stroll Ibn ʿAbd al-Barr lightly rebuked Ibn Ḥazm al-Ẓāhirī for having praised a youth they passed by because of the handsomeness of his face without awareness of any corresponding inward beauty, and the latter improvised verses defending his outward-only judgment in concordance with his literalist juristic approach.

ABŪ USĀMAH

Ḥammād b. Usāmah b. Zayd al-Qurashī by *walā'*, al-Kūfī, Abū Usāmah (d. 201 AH), he was a narrator used by the author of all the six most famous hadith compilations. He took hadith (copiously) from Hishām b. ʿUrwah, as well as from al-Aʿmash, Shuʿbah, Sufyān al-Thawrī, and a multitude of other reliable transmitters. Al-Shāfiʿī, Aḥmad b. Ḥanbal, Abū Khaythamah, Abū Shaybah's two sons Abū Bakr and ʿUthmān, and Muḥammad b. ʿAbdallāh b. Numayr were among the vast array of weighty transmitters from him. Aḥmad b. Ḥanbal called him the most knowledgeable person about people's affairs in his time, and described him, in the reports from his son ʿAbdallāh (b. Aḥmad b. Ḥanbal), as hardly prone to error in his grasp of hadith, and as a sharp-witted person. He is counted among the devotees of worship and the wise sages.

ABŪ WĀ'IL

He is Shaqīq b. Salamah al-Asadī al-Kūfī, Abū Wā'il (1–82 AH). Abū Wā'il was another great hadith transmitter from (an earlier generation of) the followers, and one of the main sources of hadith transmission for al-Aʿmash. Though his lifespan did intersect with the Prophet's ﷺ he never saw him, and thus he cannot be counted among the companions even if one were to adopt the broader and more permissive view on who falls under the first generation. The lack of any companionship, even though marginal, has been explicitly underlined by the scholars. He was a resident and one of the prominent worshippers of al-Kūfah. He transmitted hadith from the four rightly-guided caliphs. He was a reliable narrator who passed away during the caliphate of ʿUmar b. ʿAbd al-ʿAzīz according to al-Wāqidī's report.

ABŪ AL-ZINĀD

ʿAbdallāh b. Dhakwān al-Qurashī al-Madanī (65–131 AH) was from the elite of hadith experts. Al-Layth b. Saʿd said: I saw Abū al-Zinād with 300 followers behind him. He pursued knowledge, *fiqh*, poetry, morphology, writing, and accounting. Sufyān al-Thawrī designated him *amīr al-mu'minīn* in hadith. Muṣʿab al-Zubayrī said he was the *faqīh* of Ahl al-Madīnah, and Mālik's debt to him is enormous. He was an intimate scholar of classical Arabic and an eloquent speaker. He passed away suddenly in al-Madīnah.

AḤMAD B. KHĀLID

Aḥmad b. Khālid b. Zayd al-Qurṭubī, Abū ʿAmr (d. 322 AH) was known as al-Jabbāb as an agnomen of attribution to the sale of wells and cisterns. He was a *ḥāfiẓ* of hadith, the Shaykh of al-Andalus in his time, and an imam in the *fiqh* of Mālik. He wrote *Musnad Mālik*, *al-Ṣalāt*, *al-īmān*, and *Qiṣaṣ al-anbiyā'*.

AL-AḤNAF B. QAYS

Al-Aḥnaf b. Qays b. Muʿāwiyah b. Ḥusayn al-Murrī al-Saʿdī al-Minqarī al-Tamīmī, Abū Baḥr (3 B.H.–72 AH) was the chief of the tribe of Tamīm, and one of the high-ranking, clever, eloquent, and brave conquerors. He is used as a paradigm of clemency or *ḥilm*, i.e., gracious restraint from chastisement or revenge though in a position to exact it. He was born in al-Baṣrah and lived in the time of the Prophet ﷺ albeit without meeting him. He approached ʿUmar during his caliphate, and ʿUmar kept him in al-Madīnah one year, before authorizing him to return to al-Baṣrah. ʿUmar wrote to Abū Mūsā al-Ashʿarī (then governor of that city) instructing him to bring al-Aḥnaf close to him, consult with him and lend his attentive ear to him. He participated in military conquests, was appointed governor of Khurāsān, and befriended the amir of al-ʿIrāq, Muṣʿab b. al-Zubayr, whom he visited in al-Kūfah where he died in his residence. Reports on him are an ocean. The works on literature, history, and geography abound with his sermons and sentences. When a man told Yaḥyā al-Barmakī (the generous and noble *wazīr* who tutored Hārūn al-Rashīd) that he was more clement than al-Aḥnaf b. Qays, Yaḥyā replied in a rebuking tone that one who credited them with what was in excess of their due was not brought closer to them [Yaḥyā and his companions or the likes]. Al-Aḥnaf is a *laqab* or agnomen based on the fact that he was afflicted with a distortion of the foot, which is called *ḥanaf* in Arabic.

As for his first name, biographers have adopted divergent views.

ʿALĪ B. MUḤAMMAD B. ʿABDALLĀH

ʿAlī b. Muḥammad b. ʿAbdallāh b. Abī Yūsuf, Abū al-Ḥasan al-Madā'inī al-Akhbārī (d. 224 or 225 AH) was a prolific writer of books, historian, transmitter of ancient Arabic poetry, and expert in relating rare accounts as well as stories and narrations or *akhbār* (whence his *laqab* or designation of al-Akhbārī). He was originally from al-Baṣrah though he took up residence in al-Madā'in (close to Baghdad on the Tigris river, a cluster of urban settlements conquered by Saʿd b. Abī Waqqāṣ ﷺ), thereby explaining his said noun of ascription, before settling down in Baghdad where he passed away. He was regarded by al-Dhahabī as not particularly strong in hadith transmission; as it was not his scholarly forte. Al-Zubayr b. Bakkār is the most renowned *muḥaddith* who transmitted from him. The great historian Ibn Taghrī Birdī described his book on history, no longer extant, as the best in its genre and the one later scholars in such field depended upon.

AL-AʿMASH

Sulaymān b. Mihrān al-Asadī (by *walā'*) [also al-Kāhilī al-Kūfī], Abū Muḥammad (61–138 AH) was a reliable imam and high-ranking follower (from the younger generation of the followers). He was born, grew up, and died in al-Kūfah, though his ancestry linked him to Tabrestan. He was knowledgeable in Qur'ān and hadith, and transmitted 1,300 *aḥādīth*. Al-Dhahabī termed him as a leader in beneficial knowledge and salutary action alike. Al-Sakhāwī mentioned that the sultans, kings, and wealthy people were not seen as possessing a lower status in any circle of learning than in al-Aʿmash's circle, and that in spite of his extreme material want and his poverty. Aḥmad b. Ḥanbal valued the hadith transmission of Manṣūr as being more accurately reliable than al-Aʿmash's. That is due to the latter's inadvertent *tadlīs*, which in the technical nomenclature of the *muḥaddithīn* entails the concealment of a defect in the narrative chain while robing the outward of such chain with a good appearance (and thus beautifying it to the listener). If that emanated from him, it was unintentional and due to bona fide unawareness. It is *ḥarām* to conceive of anything else in respect of such veracious, scrupulous, and trustworthy luminary of the *dīn*, as emphasized by al-Dhahabī.

ᶜAMR B. RĀFIᶜ

The *ḥāfiẓ* ᶜAmr b. Rāfiᶜ b. al-Furāt b. Rāfiᶜ al-Bajalī al-Qazwīnī, Abū Ḥujr (d. 237 AH) was used as a narrator by Ibn Mājah. He transmitted from Jarīr b. ᶜAbd al-Ḥamīd, Sufyān b. ᶜUyaynah, ᶜAbdallāh b. al-Mubārak, and others. Ibn Mājah and Abū Zurᶜah were among those who transmitted from him. Abū Ḥātim reckoned him as one of the soundest *muḥaddithūn* he and his fellow students wrote narrations from.

AL-ḌAḤḤĀK B. SUFYĀN

A companion, he is al-Ḍaḥḥāk b. Sufyān b ᶜAwf b. Kaᶜb b. Abī Bakr b. Kilāb, al-Kilābī, Abū Saᶜīd.Saᶜīd b. al-Musayyib transmitted from him, and al-Ḥasan al-Baṣrī related one hadith from him. The Prophet ﷺ sent him to the tribe of Banū Kilāb to collect their taxes.

AL-DĀRAQUṬNĪ

ᶜAlī b. ᶜUmar b. Aḥmad b. Mahdī, Abū al-Ḥasan al-Shāfiᶜī (306–385 AH) was the imam in hadith of his epoch. He was born in a suburb of Baghdad called Dār al-Quṭn (lit., the Abode of Cotton). After a significant sojourn in Egypt he returned to Baghdad where he died. *Al-Sunan* is his most famous work.

AL-FUḌAYL

Al-Fuḍayl b. ᶜIyāḍ al-Tamīmī al-Yarbūᶜī (a noun of tribal attribution), Abū ᶜAlī (105–187 A.H) was a reliable transmitter of hadith, many including al-Shāfiᶜī having narrated from him. He was the Shaykh of the Makkan Ḥaram and one of the elite of righteous men of frequent devotional worship, He was born in Samarqand and came to al-Kūfah (the city of his ancestors) at an advanced age. From there he moved to Makkah where he passed away.

AL-JAWHARĪ

He is Ismāᶜīl b. Ḥammād al-Jawharī, Abū Naṣr (d. 393 AH), an imam in knowledge of the Arabic language, whose most famous work is *al-Ṣaḥḥāḥ*, incorrectly referred to by some as *al-Ṣiḥāḥ*. [A famous abridgment thereof by the linguist al-Rāzī, *Mukhtār al-ṣaḥḥāḥ*, is a standard small-sized dictionary of classical Arabic.] He was originally from Fārāb in the region of Khurāsān, like the great philosopher. After much travelling in the most renowned lands of the Islamic East, he settled in Naysābūr (Nishapur). He was the first who attempted flying and died in the path of such endeavor. He constructed two wooden boards, which he tied to a mountain, whereupon he climbed the roof of his house, calling out to the people: "I have devised something unprecedented, and I shall now fly at once." The people of Nishapur crowded to the scene, looking at him; he placed the two boards under his armpits and jumped. His invention, however, betrayed him and he fell on the ground lifeless.

AL-MUḤĀSIBĪ

Al-Ḥārith b. Asad al-Muḥāsibī, Abū ʿAbdallāh (d. 243 AH) was one of the choice Sufi masters, an admonisher easily moved to tears, who was well-versed in the fundamentals of the *dīn* as well as the *fiqh* of human transactions. He is the author of a sizeable opus, made up of works on *zuhd* and other subjects, and he taught most of the sages of Baghdad during his time. His *madhhab* in Sufism is extremely demanding (he ended up accounting for every single breath of his life, whence the agnomen he is renowned by), such that it has proven hard to follow by his successors. He was born and bred in al-Baṣrah but died in Baghdad.

AL-MUKHTĀR B. ABĪ ʿUBAYDILLĀH

Al-Mukhtār b. Abī ʿUbayd b. Masʿūd al-Thaqafī, Abū Isḥāq (1–67 AH) was one of the leading rebels against Umayyad rule, and a man of exceptional bravery. From al-Ṭā'if, he came to al-Madīnah with his father at the time of ʿUmar's caliphate. His father moved to the ʿIrāq where he died a *shahīd*. He stayed on in al-Madīnah, as a devoted supporter of the Hashemites. ʿAbdallāh b. ʿUmar b. al-Khaṭṭāb married his [Abū Isḥāq's] sister Ṣafiyyah bint Abī ʿUbayd. Al-Mukhtār, too, eventually moved to the ʿIrāq, on ʿAlī's side, and after the latter's assassination he settled in al-Baṣrah. When al-Ḥusayn b. ʿAlī was killed, al-Mukhtār turned away from the amir of al-Baṣrah, ʿUbaydullāh b. Ziyād, who managed however to have him apprehended, flogged and jailed, later exiling him to al-Ṭā'if due to the intercession of his brother-in-law ʿAbdallāh b. ʿUmar. When Yazīd b. Muʿāwiyah passed away, and ʿAbdallāh b. al-Zubayr (b. al-ʿAwwām) lay title to the caliphate, al-Mukhtār accosted him, pledged him his loyal support, fought with him for a while, then sought his authorization to head for al-Kūfah to rally support for his claim to the caliphate, which was granted in exchange for solemn assurances and conditional on clear instructions. While in al-Kūfah, however, he devoted his energy to his real concern, i.e., exacting full revenge from those who fought against and killed al-Ḥusayn. He thus summoned the people to the Imamate of Muḥammad b. al-Ḥanīfah, and secured a secret *bayʿah* of roughly

17,000 men, by whom he waged war against the governor of al-Kūfah ʿAbdallāh b. Muṭīʿ, overpowering him in the process. He seized control of Mosul (al-Mawṣil) and his political stature grew exponentially. From such a position of strength he started pursuing the killers of al-Ḥusayn, and succeeded in executing Shamir (one of those who had carried out the treacherous deed), Khawlī (who carried al-Ḥusayn's head to al-Kūfah), and ʿUmar b. Saʿd b. Abī Waqqāṣ (the general of the army that fought al-Ḥusayn). His next target was ʿUbaydullāh b. Ziyād (who had equipped the army assigned to fighting al-Ḥusayn). ʿUbaydullāh and many of those who played a role in the murder of al-Ḥusayn were killed by al-Mukhtār's troops. Al-Mukhtār used to send money to ʿAbdallāh b. ʿUmar, ʿAbdallāh b. ʿAbbās, and Muḥammad b. al-Ḥanīfah, all of whom accepted his monetary grants. Many lies about him, some of them utterly far-fetched in their character assassination, were spread by storytellers. Al-Mukhtār came to know that ʿAbdallāh b. al-Zubayr had adopted harsh measures against ʿAbdallāh b. ʿAbbās and Muḥammad b. al-Ḥanīfah for their refusal to pledge the oath of allegiance to him in al-Madīnah, and had detained the pair in a place in Makkah, from which they were released (setting out thereafter for al-Ṭā'if) by a battalion al-Mukhtār dispatched to storm Makkah for that purpose, an action which found favor with the people. ʿAbdallāh's fraternal deputy, Muṣʿab b. al-Zubayr, entered into a series of hostilities with al-Mukhtār's forces, resulting in al-Mukhtār's confinement to the palace of al-Kūfah, and the killing of both al-Mukhtār and his captured supporters. Replete with momentous events as it might have been, al-Mukhtār's emirate lasted no more than sixteen months. ʿAbd al-Malik b. ʿUmar mentioned the following odd coincidence: He saw ʿUbaydullāh b. Ziyād to whom al-Ḥusayn's head was taken; then he saw al-Mukhtār when ʿUbaydullāh's head was taken; then he witnessed al-Mukhtār's head brought to Muṣʿab b. al-Zubayr; and finally he was there when Muṣʿab's head was carried to ʿAbd al-Malik b. Marwān.

AL-SHAʿBĪ

ʿĀmir b. Sharāḥīl al-Shaʿbī (from Shaʿb, a clan of the Hamdān tribe) al-Ḥimyarī, Abū ʿAmr (19-103 AH) was a follower turned into the paradigm of excellent memorization by a proverbial saying. He was born, grew up and died (suddenly) in al-Kūfah. He associated closely with the revered Umayyad Caliph ʿAbd al-Malik b. Marwān (26–86 AH), becoming his intimate, his confidant, and his favorite sitting companion during night conversations, as well as his envoy to the Byzantine king. Physically, he was lean and emaciated, having been born at seven months, a premature child. He was asked about the extent of his memorization and replied that he put down nothing black on white, and no man narrated to him a hadith, but that he memorized it. He was a reliable transmitter and expert of Prophetic sayings. The Caliph ʿUmar b. ʿAbd al-ʿAzīz appointed him as judge, and he was a *faqīh* and poet as well.

AL-SHIBLĪ

Abū Bakr al-Shiblī, whose first name was probably (given the abundant controversy surrounding it) Dulaf b. Jaḥdar (247–334 AH) was the devoted worshipper and one of the early masters of Sufism, when Sufism was a reality without a name. Originally from Khurāsān, his ancestry being from the village of Shiblah, he was at first a governor appointed by the Abbasid authority, before he relinquished office and devoted himself to worship, achieving widespread fame for his righteousness. He was an excellent poet as well, all the poems traceable to him having been compiled in a collection or *dīwān* published in the modern era. He died in Baghdad.

AL-ṬABARĀNĪ, SULAYMĀN B. AḤMAD

Sulaymān b. Aḥmad b. Ayyūb b. Muṭayr al-Lakhmī al-Shāmī al-Ṭabarānī, Abū al-Qāsim (260–360 AH) was one of the topmost traditionists from Greater Syria, characterized by longevity and a passion for travelling. He died in Isfahan. He compiled three *maʿājim* of hadith: *al-Muʿjam al-kabīr, al-Muʿjam al-awsaṭ*, and *al-Muʿjam al-ṣaghīr*, the last-mentioned one based sequentially on the alphabetical order of his teachers' names. He authored a book on "firsts," *al-Awā'il*, of which we translated the first section, as part of a multi-volume effort to translate the whole of it in an edited, annotated, comprehensive and peculiar, multi-discipline format.

AL-TIRMIDHĪ AL-ḤAKĪM, ABŪ ʿABDALLĀH

Muḥammad b. ʿAlī b. al-Ḥasan b. Bishr, Abū ʿAbdallāh, al-Ḥakīm al-Tirmidhī (d. circa 320 AH), not to be confounded with the author of the *Sunan* (d. ca. 320 AH). He was a researcher and an analytical Sufi, well-versed in the sciences of hadith and the fundamentals of the *dīn* as well. He was from Tirmidhī from which he was banished for penning a work running counter to the prevailing views of its scholars, who went to the extreme of attesting to his presumed unbelief. Another interpretation is that the accusation of a Sufi path founded on allusions and the allegation of *kashf* or the inspirational unveiling of the unseen was levelled at his person, paving the way for his exile. A third opinion is that he was criticized for giving preference to *wilāyah* over prophethood, an accusation from which subsequent scholars defended him. Yet a fourth exegesis is that he maintained that there was a seal of the *awliyā'* in the same way as with the prophets. Having left Tirmidhī he took up residence in Balkh (possibly when he was around 90 years of age), where he was welcomed for his concordance with their prevailing *madhhab*, as reported by al-Subkī. Amongst his several works is *Nawādir al-uṣūl fī aḥādīth al-Rasūl*, which has been published. His most controversial opus is *Khatm al-wilāyah wa ʿilal al-sharīʿah*.

AL-ZUBAYR B. BAKKĀR

The Imam al-Zubayr b. Bakkār b. ʿAbdallāh al-Qurashī al-Asadī al-Makkī (172–256 AH), Abū ʿAbdallāh, was a descendant of the noble companion al-Zubayr b. al-ʿAwwām. He was a genealogist, a historian, and a transmitter of ancient Arabic poetry as well as Prophetic hadith (described in that respect as a reliable receptacle of knowledge). Born in al-Madīnah, he was appointed judge in Makkah where he died. He authored a number of significant works, some of which have been published. One of them, *al-Muwaffaqiyyāt*, was written for al-Muwaffaq b. al-Mutawkkil al-ʿAbbāsī (Ṭalḥah b. Jaʿfar b. al-Muʿtaṣim), the political leader (and de facto caliph for a period) whose tutor he was in his youth.

AL-ZUHRĪ

Muḥammad b. Muslim b. ʿAbdallāh b. Shihāb al-Zuhrī, from the Qurayshī sub-tribe of Zuhrīh b. Kilāb, Abū Bakr (58–124 AH) was one of the topmost *huffāẓ* and *fuqahā'* of the followers, and the first one to formally record the Prophetic hadith. He lived in al-Madīnah, before moving to Greater Syria where he settled (though he seemingly passed away in Shaghb, on the border between the Ḥijāz and Palestine). He memorized 2,200 *aḥādīth*. He used to bring along material (such as tablets and scrolls) on which he would write down every hadith he heard. The debt owed to him by Mālik, nay, by the custodians of the *dīn* generally, is enormous and incalculable. The great Caliph ʿUmar b. ʿAbd al-ʿAzīz wrote to his officials: "You have to take by Ibn Shihāb, since none is more knowledgeable about the Sunnah of the past than him."

ḤAMMĀD

Ḥammād b. Zayd b. Dirham al-Azdī al-Jahḍamī (a tribal ascription) al-Baṣrī al-Azraq (the dark-colored one, from "blueness," his *laqab*), Abū Ismāʿīl (98–179

AH), a sage of dignified bearing and humility, blessed with intelligence and a discerning, illuminated heart, was used by all the compilers of *al-Sittah*. A prolific hadith-narrator and a proof, he transmitted from a rich sample of the followers (such as Hishām b. ʿUrwah) and erudite scholars from the following generation. He has been lauded as the most knowledgeable man in the Sunnah and the hadith of his time [Ibn Mahdī], the one with the best juristic understanding in al-Baṣrah [Ibn Mahdī again], the unmatched *ḥāfiẓ* [Yaḥyā b. Yaḥyā al-Naysābūrī], the one with the best understanding of Islam [Abū ʿĀsim], and the master of the Muslims at the time of his death [Yazīd b. Zurayī]. Suffice it to mention in praise of him that when Mālik was once visited by one of Ḥammād's fellow townsmen, he asked about none from the people of al-Baṣrah save Ḥammād b. Zayd.

ḤĀTIM AL-RĀZĪ

His father was Muḥammad b. Idrīs b. al-Mundhir b. Dāwud b. Mihrān al-Ḥanẓalī, Abū Ḥātim (195–277 AH), a *ḥāfiẓ* of hadith, among the contemporaries of al-Bukhārī and Muslim. He was born in al-Rayy, in the Khurāsānī region (the noun of ascription whereto is al-Rāzī), and died in Baghdad after manifold relocations in disparate regions, sometimes far away from one another. He penned several worthy works [Abū Ḥātim al-Rāzī]. The reference here is to his son ʿAbd al-Raḥmān (240–327 AH), Abū Muḥammad, the prominent *ḥāfiẓ* of hadith and the author of the key reference work in the science of hadith narrators *al-Jarḥ wa al-taʿdīl* [Ibn Abī Ḥātim].

HISHĀM B. ʿAMMĀR

Hishām b. ʿAmmār al-Sulamī, Abū al-Walīd (153–245 AH) was a judge and a renowned Qur'ānic reciter, described by al-Dhahabī as the *khaṭīb*, Qur'ānic reciter, *muḥaddith*, and *ʿālim* of his city Damascus, where he died.

HISHĀM B. ʿURWAH

ʿUrwah b. al-Zubayr's son, Abū al-Mundhir (61–146 AH) was a follower (of the younger generation). He was one of the imams in hadith, and one of the *ʿulamā'* of al-Madīnah, where he was born and lived. He visited al-Kūfah, and its residents took knowledge from him, then he came to Baghdad (where he eventually died) on a visit to the Abbasid ruler al-Manṣūr, one of whose elite advisers he was. Around 400 *aḥādīth* have been narrated by him, and accounts of his life, sayings and deeds are countless.

IBN ABĪ KHAYTHAMAH

Aḥmad b. Zuhayr (Abī Khaythamah) b. Ḥarb b. Shaddād al-Nasā'ī then al-Baghdādī, Abū Bakr (185–279 AH) was a historian and one of the *ḥuffāẓ* of hadith. He was a reliable scholar and a narrator of works of literature. His ancestry was from Nasā (whence his first noun of ascription), though he was born and died in Baghdad (thereby explaining his second such noun). His most illustrious work, *al-Tārīkh al-kabīr*, was praised by al-Dāraquṭnī as the most copiously beneficial work on history.

IBN LAHĪʿAH

ʿAbdallāh b. Lahīʿah b. Fur'ān (or b. ʿUqbah) al-Haḍramī al-Miṣrī, Abū ʿAbd al-Raḥmān (97-174 AH) was the judge, *ʿālim*, and *muḥaddith* of the Egyptian lands. Aḥmad b. Ḥanbal affirmed that Egypt had no *muḥaddith* but Ibn Lahīʿah. And Sufyān al-Thawrī averred that the roots were found with Ibn Lahīʿah, and the branches with him and his likes. In the year 154 AH he was appointed judge in the service of the Abbasid ruler al-Manṣūr, who allocated to him 30 gold coins per month. He remained in that post for ten years. In 170 AH his house and private library were burnt down, so the great savant al-Layth b. Saʿd sent him 1,000 gold coins. He wrote down many *aḥādīth*, encompassed a vast knowledge in diverse fields, and travelled long and hard in quest of further knowledge. He died in Cairo. More than seven and a half pages, in what is generally a condensed work distinguished by its terseness, were consecrated to him by al-Dhahabī in *Mīzān al-iʿtidāl*. Not everybody shared Aḥmad's appreciation, and lack of strength, or positive weakness has been attributed to him by more than one expert.

IBN AL-MUBĀRAK

ʿAbdallāh b. al-Mubārak b. Wāḍiḥ al-Ḥanẓalī (by *walā'*, for he was the son of a slave, and was attached to the tribe of Ḥanẓalah via the process of setting free) al-Tamīmī al-Marwazī, Abū ʿAbd al-Rahmān (118–181 AH). He was a *ḥāfiẓ* in hadith, Shaykh al-Islām, a warrior, and a very capable trader who travelled and performed the hajj many times and composed many works, including a celebrated one on *zuhd*, *al-Raqā'iq*. He was the first scholar to write a treatise specifically about jihad, which is well-known and has been published in many editions. He was strong in *fiqh* and in Arabic history, too, and combined bravery with exceptional generosity. He died in a town on the Euphrates after a military raid against the Byzantines. The works on history and biography overflow with reports about him. He studied under both Sufyān al-Thawrī and Abū Hanīfah, extolling the virtues of both and causing the former to appreciate the latter and remove the misgivings about him sowed by what Sufyān had learnt second-hand about the Kufan Imam. When he sat one day in the circle of learning of Mālik in al-Madīnah, he seated him in a place of honor, despite his students' unawareness of his status, and at the end introduced him to his students as the "*faqīh* of Khurāsān," the region ʿAbdallāh was from originally. It is not surprising that the author quotes his definition that focuses on *zuhd* with the heart. Through his trading enterprises, he was a whirlpool of wealth-acquisition and distribution. He once said that he would not trade if it were not for the likes of al-Fuḍayl b. ʿIyāḍ, i.e., he generated wealth to sustain the worshipping of the *zuhhād*, not for self-gratification or aggrandizement.

IBN AL-MUHĀJIR

He may be Khālid b. al-Muhājir b. Sayfillāh (the great "Sword of Allāh") Khālid b. al-Walīd b. al-Mughīrah al-Makhzūmī, and Allāh knows best. If this is the case, he was a Ḥijāzī and ostensibly a staunch opponent of the Umayyads,

IBN AL-NABBĀḤ

ʿĀmir b. al-Nabbāḥ, the *mu'adhdhin* of ʿAlī b. Abī Ṭālib who also narrated *aḥādīth* from him. Cf. *Ṭabaqāt b. Saʿd.*

IBN ʿUYAYNAH

Sufyān b. ʿUyaynah b. Maymūn al-Hilālī al-Kūfī (as he was born in al-Kūfah), Abū Muḥammad (107–198 AH) was the great *muḥaddith* of the Makkan Ḥaram, who passed away in Makkah. He was a reliable *ḥāfiẓ* of hadith and a sage of vast knowledge, highly ranked by people. Al-Shāfiʿī's statement is renowned: "Were it not for Mālik and Sufyān, the knowledge of the Ḥijāz (with its two epicenters Makkah and al-Madīnah) would have vanished." He was one-eyed and performed the hajj seventy times.

IBRĀHĪM B. ADHAM

He is Ibrāhīm b. Adham b. Manṣūr al-Tamīmī al-Balkhī, Abū Isḥāq (d. 161 AH), the prestigious *zāhid* whose father was one of the affluent men in Balkh (the largest city in Khurāsān at that time), and who travelled at length in the three pivotal regions of the ʿIrāq, Greater Syria, and the Ḥijāz. He maintained himself by doing harvesting and grinding work, guarding orchards, and serving as a porter, while fighting the Byzantines in raiding platoons. His father's slave came to him once with 10,000 silver coins and the news that his deceased parent had bequeathed a huge fortune to him, whereupon he set the slave free and donated the silver coins to him, unconcerned thereafter with his father's legacy of wealth in Balkh. In winter he used to wear a fur with no shirt underneath, and in summer he wore no turban or shoes, fasting whether travelling or resident in a town. He spoke classical Arabic eloquently, so much so that if he attended a lesson by Sufyān al-Thawrī consecrated to admonishing counsel, Sufyān would shorten his talk out of fear of making any linguistic error. The anecdotes and reports about him are plentiful, though not always consistent. He possibly died in a Byzantine citadel.

IBRĀHĪM AL-NAKHAᶜĪ

Ibrāhīm b. Yazīd b. Qays b. al-Aswad, Abū ᶜImrān al-Nakhaᶜī (46–96 AH) was one of the choicest *fuqahā'* of the followers, and among their elite of veracious and righteous guides. A truthful memorizer and narrator of hadith from al-Kūfah, he passed away in a concealed place hiding away from the despotic Umayyad governor al-Ḥajjāj. He has been described as the *faqīh* of al-ᶜIrāq. He was a *mujtahid* imam in his own right, and he had his own *madhhab* which has, however, failed to survive. On his death, al-Shaᶜbī mourned the passing of an unequalled champion of good.

JAᶜFAR B. BURQĀN

Jaᶜfar b. Burqān (d. 154 AH) was the companion of Maymūn b. Mihrān and one of the *ᶜulamā'* of the ᶜIrāqī city of al-Raqqah. Wakīᶜ and Abū Nuᶜaym have *inter alia* transmitted hadith from him. He was illiterate. He is regarded as a reliable transmitter save in respect of his narrations from al-Zuhrī.

JAᶜFAR B. SULAYMĀN

He is probably al-Ḍubaᶜī (d. 178 AH), a scholar and hadith transmitter renowned for his *zuhd* but also for his quasi-Shīᶜī inclination to the Ahl al-Bayt. Al-Bukhārī reported a view that he was illiterate.

JARĪR

The judge Jarīr b. ᶜAbd al-Ḥamīd b. Qurṭ al-Ḍabbī al-Rāzī, Abū ᶜAbdallāh (110-188 AH) was born in one of the villages around Isfahan, though he grew up in al-Kūfah and settled in Rayy (whence al-Rāzī). He transmitted from al-Aᶜmash, *inter alia*, and among those who transmitted from him one can enumerate the two sons of Abū Shaybah, Abū Khaythamah, Yaḥyā b. Maᶜīn, and Yaḥyā b. Yaḥyā. Narrations from him are found in each of *al-Sittah*. He was trustworthy, a proof for Ibn ᶜAmmār al-Mawṣilī, and one to whom people used to set out in travel to receive hadith from.

KAᶜB

Kaᶜb al-Aḥbār, i.e., Kaᶜb b. Mātiᶜ al-Ḥimyarī, Abū Isḥāq (d. 32 AH), was a follower andone of the leading Jewish *ᶜulamā'* in the era of the *Jāhiliyyah*; he embraced Islam during the caliphate of Abū Bakr, and took up residence in al-Madīnah when the reins of power had been handed over to ᶜUmar. The companions, and not only they, took from him many accounts of the bygone nations, while in turn he received knowledge of the Book and the Sunnah from the companions. He eventually relocated to Greater Syria, settling in Ḥimṣ where he passed away at the venerable age of 104 years.

KAᶜB B. ᶜIYĀḌ

Kaᶜb b. ᶜIyāḍ al-Ashᶜarī was a companion from Greater Syria. Jābir b. ᶜAbdallāh and possibly Umm al-Dardā' transmitted from him. The famous narration he is associated with was related from him by Jubayr b. Nufayr al-Ḥaḍramī, another companion whose existence spanned both Jāhiliyyah and Islām.

KHĀLID AL-ḤADHDHĀ'

Khālid b. Mihrān al-Baṣrī al-Ḥadhdhā' (an agnomen meaning the shoemaker or trader in footwear), Abū al-Manāzil (d. 141 or 142 AH) was likewise used by all the authors of *al-Sittah*. He met Anas b. Mālik. He transmitted from Abū Qilābah, Muḥammad b. Sīrīn and others. Sufyān al-Thawrī, Shuᶜbah, al-Aᶜmash, and his own shaykh, Muḥammad b. Sīrīn, together with many more, transmitted from him. He was an awe-inspiring, venerable person of reliable and copious hadith transmission. He was used in al-Baṣrah to collect the taxes levied on the lands whose owners entered Islam at a time when they were the proprietors thereof. However, in the last part of his life, as reported from Ḥammād b. Zayd, his faculty of recollection changed for the worse. Yaḥyā said: I asked Ḥammād b. Zayd: "And (what about) Khālid al-Ḥadhdhā'?" He replied: "He visited us once from Greater Syria and it was as if we no longer recognized his memorization and we refuted it. Shuᶜbah wanted to reproach him, so ᶜAbbād b. ᶜAbbād decided to approach Khālid with Ḥammād b. Zayd and they said to him: What's the matter with you? Have you gone insane? The pair threatened him and he kept quiet. This science is a *dīn*, as Mālik said, so one might be a revered man of righteousness, and even an *ᶜālim* in the very field he is mercilessly but generously asked to estrange himself from, to preserve its purity, at a later stage when his proficiency dwindles and recedes.

KHAWLAH BINT QAYS

Khawlah bint Qays b. Qahd b. Qays al-Anṣārīyyah, Umm Muḥammad was a Ṣaḥābiyyah, and a wife of the conquering lion of Allāh, Ḥamzah b. ᶜAbd al-Muṭṭalib ﵁.

MAḤMŪD AL-WARRĀQ

Maḥmūd b. Ḥasan al-Warrāq (d. ca.225 AH), was a poet mostly devoted to composing works of admonition and wisdom. Ibn al-Mubarrad quoted some of his verses in *al-Kāmil fī al-lughah wa al-adab*, and his collected poetical opus or *dīwān* has been published.

MĀLIK, ABŪ YŪSUF

Abū Yūsuf Mālik was Abū Ḥanīfah's foremost disciple with al-Shaybānī.

MĀLIK B. DĪNĀR

Mālik b. Dīnār al-Baṣrī, Abū Yaḥyā (d. 131 AH) was a man of scrupulous piety who ate from the earnings of his work, and used to copy down the *muṣḥaf* of the Qur'ān in exchange for a fee (at a time when that was unusual). He was also a known hadith narrator who is buried in al-Baṣrah.

MANṢŪR

Manṣūr b. Ismāᶜīl b. ᶜUmar al-Tamīmī al-Miṣrī, Abū al-Ḥasan(d. 306 AH) was the blind poet and Shāfiᶜī jurist from Baghdad. He schooled in *fiqh* at the hands of the immediate followers of al-Shāfiᶜī and their followers. His poetry was of outstanding quality, and he was proficient in many sciences. Many stories and anecdotes about him have survived, including the accounts of his generosity to the judge Abū ᶜUbayd, as well as the friction that eventually developed between them, and the split in political partisanship to the two of them as a result thereof.

MASRŪQ

Masrūq b. al-Ajdaʿ b. Mālik al-Hamdānī al-Wādiʿī, Abū ʿĀ'ishah (d. 63 AH) was a reliable Yemeni savant from the followers, who settled in al-Madīnah during Abū Bakr's caliphate before relocating to al-Kūfah where he took part in ʿAlī's campaigns. He was more proficient in fatwa-issuing than the renowned Shurayḥ, who in turn excelled over him in judicial decision-making.

MUḤAMMAD B. ʿABDALLĀH

Muḥammad b. ʿAbdallāh b. Ḥamdawayh al-Ḍabbī al-Naysābūrī, known as al-Ḥākim, Abū ʿAbdallāh (321–405 AH) was one of the great *ḥuffāẓ* of hadith and a writer of significant works in that science. He was born and died in Nishapur (whence his noun of ascription), though he travelled extensively. He was selected for judicial appointment in Jurjān after he had been a judge in his native town as well, but he declined to accept the appointment. He received knowledge at the hands of 1,000 *shuyūkh*. He was also a good political ambassador.

MUḤAMMAD B. ISḤĀQ

Muḥammad b. Isḥāq b. Khuzaymah al-Sulamī, Abū Bakr (223–311 AH) was the Imam of Nishapur in his era. He was a jurist, a *mujtahid* and an expert of hadith, lauded by al-Subkī as the Imam of Imams; he travelled quite a lot though he was born and died in Nishapur.

MUḤAMMAD B. SĪRĪN

The follower Muḥammad b. Sīrīn al-Baṣrī al-Anṣārī (by *walā'*), Abū Bakr (33–110 AH) was the imam of his time in Islamic sciences in the city of al-Baṣrah (where he was born and died), a noble writer who grew up as a cloth merchant, and he was partly deaf. He learnt *fiqh* and narrated *aḥādīth*. He became famous for his extreme scrupulousness in the *dīn* and his interpretation of dreams, on which he authored a well-known treatise published in several editions. Another work on the subject (*Muntakhab al-kalām fī tafsīr al-aḥlām*) is misleadingly attributed to him. His father was the freed slave of Anas b. Mālik, and Anas used him as an official scribe.

MUSADDAD

Musaddad b. Musarhad b. Musarbal (b. Mugharbal b. Mura'bal b. Urandal b. Sīrīndal b. ʿUrandal) al-Baṣrī al-Asadī, Abū al-Ḥasan (d. 228 AH) was a *ḥāfiẓ* from among the *muḥaddithūn* who transmitted from Fuḍayl b. ᶜIyāḍ, Ḥammād b. Zayd and several others. Al-Bukhārī and Abū Dāwud transmitted from him. Generally praised as a reliable narrator, he was defined as a proof and one of the trustworthy imams by Ibn Nāṣir al-Dīn. He was the first to compile a *musnad* of hadith (arranged on the basis of the names of the ultimate narrators, not on subject-based chapters like prayer, *zakāt*, fasting, etc.) in al-Baṣrah. He wrote to Aḥmad b. Ḥanbal (an estimator of him) asking him details about the *fitnah* which plagued people with the dissemination of fatalist trends, over-rationalist doctrines, the false allegation of the created nature of the Qur'ān, the emergence of the Rafidites' movement and similar other topics. Aḥmad replied to him in a four-page synoptic letter.

QATĀDAH

Qatādah b. Diᶜāmah b. Qatādah b. ᶜAzīz, Abū al-Khaṭṭāb, al-Sadūsī al-Baṣrī (61–118 AH) was the renowned *mufassir* and *ḥāfiẓ* eulogized by Aḥmad b. Ḥanbal as the summit of the Baṣrīn *ḥuffāẓ*. He was also a leader in the sciences of Arabic, historical accounts of the Arabs and genealogy. He was born blind and died during the plague in Wāsiṭ, the city built by al-□ajjāj between Baghdad and al-Kūfah, so named because it lies equidistantly between al-Kūfah and al-Baṣrah, in the median point (*wasaṭ*).

SAᶜD

Saᶜd Ibn Abī Waqqāṣ.

SAᶜD B. ᶜUBĀDAH

Saᶜd b. ᶜUbādah b. Dulaym al-Anṣārī al-Sāᶜidī, Abū Thābit was a handsome nobleman and generous chief from among the Madīnan companions; he participated in the first pledge of al-ᶜAqabah and in the Battle of Badr according to some historians such as al-Wāqidī (but not Ibn Isḥāq). He continuously fed people with meat and fats, following in the tradition of his father ᶜUbādah and his grandfather Dulaym. His own son Qays, in turn, used to summon his fellow townsmen to the same, and was renowned for his exceptional liberality as well.

SAHL B. AL-ḤANẒALIYYAH

He is Sahl b. al-Rabīᶜ b. ᶜAmr b. ᶜAdiyy b. Zayd al-Anṣārī, from the tribe of al-Aws, one of the two largest Madīnan tribes (al-Ḥanẓaliyyah being his mother, though it is also said his great grandmother). He took part in the oath of allegiance under the tree, and was a virtuous man of knowledge who shunned people's company and sitting together with them, while praying and remembering Allāh frequently. He relocated to Greater Syria, meeting his death in Damascus, without leaving behind any offspring, in the early part of Muʿāwiyah's caliphate. Apparently, he was biologically prevented from fathering a child, but he was not bothered by that, declaring to Saʿīd b. ʿAbd al-ʿAzīz that having any base, low-value chattel or foodstuff coming his way while on the *dīn* was dearer to him than whatever the sun rose on.

SAHL B. MUʿĀDH

Sahl b. Muʿādh b. Anas al-Juhanī transmitted from his father. Yaḥyā b. Maʿīn declared him weak, whereas Ibn Ḥibbān wavered about his evaluation.

SAHL B. SAʿD AL-SĀʿIDĪ

He is Sahl b. Saʿd al-Khazrajī al-Anṣārī (d. 91 AH) from the tribe of Banū Sāʿidah (reflected in his aforementioned noun of ascription). He was a celebrated Madīnan companion who lived around 100 years, transmitting 188 *aḥādīth* reported in the collections of Prophetic sayings.

SAHL AL-ṢUʿLŪKĪ

Sahl b. Muḥammad b. Sulaymān al- Ṣuʿlūkī al-Naysābūrī, Abū al-Ṭayyib (d. 387 AH) was the Ḥanafī jurisprudent from the region of Khurāsān and the mufti of Nishapur in his time, as well as the son of the previous mufti thereof. His renowned work is *al-Fawā'id*.

SAʿĪD B. AL-MUSAYYIB

Saʿīd b. al-Musayyib b. Ḥazn b. Abī Wahb al-Makhzūmī al-Qurashī, Abū Muḥammad (13–94 AH) was one of the elite of the followers, nay, the Master of the Followers (Sayyid al-Tābiʿīn). He was one of the seven *fuqahā'* of al-Madīnah, his resting place, a treasure of *fiqh*, hadith, *zuhd*, and scrupulousness in the *dīn*; he lived out of trade in oil and accepted no grant from the political authorities. He knew better than anybody else the judgments and rulings of ʿUmar b. al-Khaṭṭāb, to such an extent that he was nicknamed *rāwiyatu* ʿUmar, the one who transmitted and preserved ʿUmar's legacy. Not surprisingly, Mālik's connection to him was indissoluble.

SAᶜĪD B. SULAYMĀN AL-WĀSIṬĪ

Saᶜīd b. Sulaymān al-Ḍabbī al-Wāsiṭī al-Bazzāz, Abū ᶜUthmān (d. 225 AH), known as Saᶜdawayh, was a resident of Baghdad. He was used, directly and indirectly, by the compilers of *al-Sittah* without exception, and was a reliable narrator praised by the bulk of experts. He died in Baghdad in the year 225 AH, at the age of 100.

SHAQĪQ

Shaqīq al-Balkhī, i.e., Shaqīq b. Ibrāhīm b. ᶜAlī al-Azdī al-Balkhī, Abū ᶜAlī (d. 194 AH) was a famous *zāhid* and Sufi and one of the venerable shaykhs of Khurāsān in his age and thereafter. It is speculated that he might have been the first to speak methodically on the knowledge of Sufi states in the region of Khurāsān. He was one of the prominent *mujāhids* as well, and died as *shahīd* in a military expedition.

SUFYĀN AL-THAWRĪ

Sufyān b. Saᶜīd b. Masrūq al-Thawrī (97–161 AH) was from the tribe of Banū Thawrīb. ᶜAbd Manāt branching off from Muḍar. His *kunyā* was Abū ᶜAbdallāh. He was born and bred in al-Kūfah. He was *amīr al-mu'minīn* in hadith and the master of the people of his epoch in knowledge of the sciences of the *dīn* as well as in *taqwā*. His *madhhab* was one of the renowned ones in the Islamic lands for a long period, though it eventually became extinct due to the lack of eminent followers who, uninterruptedly, recorded, studied, and transmitted it, thereby preserving it for posterity. He was sought after to take charge of the judicial affairs of the caliph by two Abbasid rulers, al-Manṣūr and al-Mahdī, but he declined the overtures of both. In the first case, he left al-Kūfah to sojourn in Makkah and al-Madīnah. With the latter, he hid away and relocated to al-Baṣrah where he passed away in concealment. Among his famous sayings was the following: "I never memorized something that I later forgot."

ṬALḤAH

Ṭalḥah fought in the Battle of Uḥud), and was bleeding profusely and lying wounded in one of the groves after he sustained nearly seventy wounds and blows and lost his fingers during the battle. On top of his selfless courage, he had to wait for nursing while care was taken first of the Prophet ﷺ. After the battle, when the Prophet ﷺ stood on the *minbar* in the mosque of al-Madīnah, a verse was revealed praising the men from the *mu'minun* who were true to the covenant they made with Allah, some of them having fulfilled their pact by death and some others still waiting to do so, not having changed in any way at all [Sūrah al-Aḥzāb, 33:23], someone stood up and asked: "O Messenger of Allāh, who are such people?" At that moment, as recounted by Abū Bakr [cf. *Ḥilyat al-awliyā'*], Ṭalḥah had just arrived at the mosque, wearing a green robe under a green cloak, when the Messenger of Allāh ﷺ saw him, he said: "O questioner, here is one of them."

TAMĪM AL-DĀRĪ

Tamīm b. Aws b. Khārijah al-Dārī, Abū Ruqayyah was an illustrious companion who embraced Islam in the ninth year after the Hijrah. He lived in al-Madīnah, which he left for Greater Syria after the assassination of ʿUthmān, settling in Jerusalem and dying in Palestine. He was a devoted worshipper who led an ascetic life; he was the foremost exponent of such practices in Palestine during his time. He was the first to keep a light burning continually in a mosque, a constant practice of the Muslims up to the present days.

THĀBIT

When the name Thābit, without further elaboration, is cited, the reference is to Thābit b. Aslam al-Bunānī al-Baṣrī, Abū Muḥammad (d. 123 or 127 AH), a righteous man and trustworthy transmitter. He was extolled by Abū Ḥātim as the most reliable of the students who associated with Anas b. Mālik and narrated from him, save for al-Zuhrī, and preferred even to Qatādah in that regard. He spent forty years in the company of Anas, he used to recite the Qur'ān day and night, and to fast assiduously. Al-Muzanī said he had met no more devout worshipper than him. He was, among the inhabitants of al-Baṣrah, one of the pillars of sincere worship.

ʿUMĀRAH B. ZĀDĀN

He is ʿUmārah b. Zādān al-Baṣrī al-Ṣaydalānī, Abū Salamah. Some critics of narrators, however, held a better view of his status.

UMM AYMAN

Barakah b. Thaʿlabah was the servant and wet nurse of the Prophet ﷺ who was first married to ʿUbayd al-Ḥabashī, from whose union she had Ayman (known as Ibn Umm Ayman), and then to Zayd b. Ḥārithah, giving birth to his son Usāmah. Accounts on this great woman proliferate. She took part in both migrations, to Abyssinia and to al-Madīnah. She was under ʿAbdallāh b. ʿAbd al-Muṭṭalib, and was transferred to the Prophet ﷺ by inheritance. It is also said she was under the mother of the Prophet ﷺ who termed her "my mother after my mother." He used to visit her in her house, as did Abū Bakr and ʿUmar after him ﷺ. She is, according to one view, the one who in the famous narration informed the inquiring Prophet ﷺ that she had drank his urine from the bowl he ﷺ had placed under his bed.

UMM KULTHŪM BINT ʿUQBAH

Umm Kulthūm bint ʿUqbah b. Abī Muʿīṭ [Abān b. Abī ʿAmr] embraced Islam in Makkah before the women started to migrate to al-Madīnah. She herself made hijrah and gave formal allegiance to the Prophet ﷺ (and thus falls under the description *al-muhājirāt al-mubāyiʿāt* in Sūrah al-Mumtaḥanah). It has also been reported that she was the first woman to migrate to al-Madīnah, in the year 7 AH, during the truce between the Prophet ﷺ and the *mushrikūn* of Quraysh. Since they had stipulated with the Prophet ﷺ that any believing woman who came to al-Madīnah from Makkah had to be returned to them, the famous verse in the selfsame chapter came down with the new legislation of the issue. Upon her migration, in fact, her two brothers al-Walīd and ʿUmārah, ʿUqbah's sons, accosted her with a view to returning her to the associationists (as per the said divinely abrogated agreement), but Allāh forbade such occurrence by the revelation of the said verse, by virtue of her Islam. Many accounts of this remarkable woman's life have survived. It is said that she walked from Makkah to al-Madīnah. She first married Zayd b. Ḥārithah, then, after he was killed, al-Zubayr b. al-ʿAwwām, and thereafter, subsequent to his divorcing her, ʿAbd al-Raḥmān b. ʿAwf, with whom she gave birth to two or three sons. She outlived him. She then married ʿAmr b. al-ʿĀṣ, with whom she spent one month before meeting her death. She was ʿUthmān's half-sister (through his mother).

ʿURWAH B. AL-ZUBAYR

He is one of the seven *fuqahā'* of al-Madīnah and the son of the lofty companion al-Zubayr b. al-ʿAwwām, al-Asadī al-Qurashī, Abū ʿAbdallāh (22–93 AH). A stalwart of the followers, righteous, generous, knowledgeable about the *dīn*, he steered clear of any political or religious *fitnah* stirring up the Islamic community of his age. He moved first to al-Baṣrah and subsequently to Egypt, where he married and resided for seven years, returning thereafter to al-Madīnah, his final resting place. He was the full brother of ᶜAbdallāh b. al-Zubayr. The well called Bi'r ᶜUrwah in al-Madīnah takes its name from him.

UWAYS AL-QARANĪ

Uways b. ᶜĀmir b. Jaz' b. Mālik al-Qaranī was from the Banū Qaran b. Radmān (d. 37 AH) was one of the masters of the followers, as well as one of the great ascetics and devout worshippers of the early part of this ummah. He was originally from the Yemen. He used to dwell in desert wastelands and amidst sand-dunes. He was born during the time of the Prophet ﷺ but did not see him. He went to meet ᶜUmar b. al-Khaṭṭab before residing temporarily in al-Kūfah. He participated in the battle of Ṣiffīn with ᶜAlī, and the predominant opinion of the historians is that he passed away in such battle.

WUHAYB B. AL-WARD

Wuhayb b. al-Ward b. Abī al-Ward al-Makhzūmī (by *walā'*), Abū Umayyah (d. 153 AH) was a contemporary of Ibrāhīm b. Adham and one of the prominent devout worshippers and wise savants. His name was ᶜAbd al-Wahhāb, which by a morphological process of diminution turned into Wuhayb. He was originally from Makkah, and died there. Whenever Sufyān al-Thawrī transmitted hadith in the Masjid al-Ḥarām in Makkah, he would say to the people, on completion thereof: "Go (now) to the pleasantly wholesome," meaning Wuhayb. Reports and statements of his have been preserved.

ZĀ'IDAH

He is, correctly, Zā'idah b. Qudāmah al-Thaqafī al-Kūfī, Abū Ṣalt (d. 160 or 161 AH), who transmitted from al-Aᶜmash and from whom, in turn, Abū Usāmah transmitted narrations. He was regarded as truthful and a man of knowledge by Abū Zurᶜah, and as a reliable narrator and a broad embodiment of the Sunnah by Abū Ḥātim and al-ᶜIjlī. Al-Nasā'ī, Ibn Saᶜd, Ibn Hibbān, and al-Dāraquṭnī, too, had a high opinion of him. He died in Byzantine country during a military expedition.

NOTES

1. See Ibn Khaldūn's *al-Muqaddimah.*

2. Literally: *Tawajjuh*, i.e., orientation, or setting his face towards something, with the meaning here in all likelihood of the orientation to earn a sufficient modicum for his daily existence, without letting that consume too much of his time or subtract vital space from his said two other central pursuits.

3. Cf. al-Qurṭubī's own *tafsīr, al-Jāmiᶜ fī aḥkām al-Qur'ān.*

4. Ibid.

5. *Zahida* is obviously the *māḍī, yazhadu* the *muḍāri', fī* and *ᶜan* are the letters by which it takes its indirect object, and *zuhd / zahādah* two forms the *maṣdar* (original) of the verb assumes. Another variant which has been mentioned by the linguists is *zahad.*

6. Literally, another "language" of the Arabs in the pronunciation of the verb, since it has been transmitted that they made authentic use of such alternative form. Thaᶜlab, another prominent linguist, records the existence of the variant *zahuda* as well.

7. The *maṣdar*, i.e., carrying out, generally and without correlation to time, the act of the verb *tazahhada.*

8. That is the equivalent of the noun of the doer of the augmented verbal form *azhada* of the *afᶜala* morphological type. Since no action but a status is expressed by the verb, there is no "doer" as such, but a person endowed with

the qualitative status of possessing scant financial means.

9.   Cf. *al-Jāmiʿ al-ṣaghīr* by al-Suyūṭī. Al-Suyūṭī ascribed it to al-Daylamī in the transmission from Abū Hurayrah, and marked it with the symbol indicating a weak (*ḍaʿīf*) hadith. The meaning of the hadith is: a believer with little wealth, since he exercises *zuhd* in what he possesses due to its paucity. The adjectival attribute *muzhad* (on such reading of the relevant word) is the equivalent of the noun of the patient (not the doer), i.e., one in respect of whom others exercise *zuhd*. Because of his poverty and ragged clothes, he is not given consideration and weight, and people's attention is not directed to him. Others have transmitted the report on the basis that the word used is *muzhid*, the noun of the doer, from the verb *azhada fi al-dunyā* (he exercises *zuhd* in this worldly existence) whenever the slave relinquishes this World. The believer's *zuhd* in this World, in fact, makes him attain the highest degrees in the otherworldly life. Accordingly, when ʿĪsā 𐎠 was asked about two men who chanced upon a treasure, one of whom bypassed it without bothering to give it any attention while the other seized it, as to who was the better of the two, he replied: "The one who left it aside." That has been narrated by al-Munāwī in his commentary on al-Suyūṭī's said collection, titled *Fayḍ al-qadīr*, which the readers are referred to concerning this whole hadith.

10.   See in this entire regard the entry "*zāy-hā'-dāl*" in *Lisān al-ʿArab* by the great African linguist Ibn Manẓūr.

11.   There are a number of companions with such *kunyā*. The reference is here to the most copious narrator of Prophetic sayings among them, Ṣudayy b. ʿAjlān al-Bāhilī, from the tribe of Bāhilah. He settled eventually in Egypt, and later in the city of Ḥimṣ in Greater Syria (al-Shām), where he passed away in the year 81 AH He was, according to some, the last companion to die in Greater Syria. Not surprisingly, the hadith transmitters from al-Shām have particularly relied on his narrations.

12.   It has been reported by al-Tirmidhī in his *Sunan*, by Aḥmad b. Ḥanbal in his *Musnad*, and by al-Baghawī in *al-Mishkāt*, i.e., *Mishkāt al-maṣābīḥ*.

13.   It is not our intention here to delve into the subtleties of hadith classification. Suffice it to point out that in the technical lexicon of al-Tirmidhī, the unqualified *ḥasan* hadith coincides with what has been described by the experts in this science as *ḥasan li ghairih*, i.e., good in other than itself, meaning

the weak one with several narrative chains, the plurality of which cure its feebleness when examined on its own.

14.   In other words, the author repudiates the focus on the said exalted duo of companions as representing (negative) exceptions to the widespread practice of *zuhd* in the era of the best generation. He rebuts such claim with concrete and detailed counter-proof in subsequent chapters.

15.   The author being on his *madhhab*.

16.   And thus, without falling into sinfulness being in issue, it is nevertheless preferable to stick to those neutrally permissible matters untainted by any obfuscating doubt, and do away with the rest.

17.   Al-Musayyib b. Wāḍiḥ, al-Sulamī al-Talmannasī (from a fortress in Greater Syria) al-Ḥimṣī. He transmitted hadith from Ibn al-Mubārak and others, and inter alia Abū Ḥātim transmitted from him in turn. He used to write down *aḥādīth* himself. Al-Nasāʾī had a high opinion of him as a narrator, others esteemed him less. Abū Ḥātim himself mentioned that he was a truthful transmitter who used to err a lot in what he transmitted.

18.   In his *tafsīr*, the author commented that Sufyān 🕮 had spoken the truth, since the one whose hope is restrained does not seek the most pleasantly wondrous foodstuffs and a variegated diversity of clothes, and takes from this World what has been made easy to him of it, contented with the measure thereof which ensures sufficiency.

19.   One of the followers who took from him. He is obviously relating a true dream that occurred to him after Sufyān's death.

20.   Rephrasing the question better.

21.   *Al-riḍā*, satisfaction, pleasure with one's lot.

22.   In his *tafsīr*, al-Qurṭubī traced such statement to al-Awzāʾī and those who took that same definitional path.

23.   The "I" is the first person of the author, al-Qurṭubī. "This" refers to the last-mentioned statement of al-Thawrī preceding the view of "some people."

24.   The *kunyā*, i.e., patronymic name of Jaʿfar b. Sulaymān.

25.   In his *tafsīr*, he quoted from Fuḍayl the other statement that *zuhd* meant to renounce the whole of this World, whether one liked such renunciation

or not. He then proceeded to mention the saying of Bishr b. al-Ḥārith that love of this World was love of meeting people, and *zuhd* in this World lay in doing without meeting people, following that up with a third citation from Fuḍayl, to the effect that he said: "The distinguishing sign of *zuhd* in this World is to do without people—make *zuhd* of people."

26. That is, is a true *zāhid*.

27. That is, turning away from wealth and fame, and being the opposite of desire.

28. Meaning ostensibly the grandson of the Prophet ﷺ.

29. In his *tafsīr*, he contended that the definition of *zuhd* as the circumscription of hope was the most general in the meaning it engirded, and was the worthiest and most appropriate one.

30. That is, his *Sunan*.

31. Cf. al-Tirmidhī's *Sunan*, Ibn Mājah's *Sunan*, and *al-Mishkāt* by al-Baghawī. The meaning of the hadith is that you are rewarded for the calamity but such reward would go amiss should you not be struck by it. Two reliable witnesses of your *zuhd* in this World and your inclination to the final destination in the Afterlife are thus to have greater desire in the occurrence and existence of the calamity for the sake of its reward than your desire for its non-existence.

32. That is, the one transmitted from Abū Dharr.

33. In a nutshell, such a hadith is for him one which the experts of hadith have found to be strange for one of several possible reasons, such as the addition found in a transmission compared to the other narrative variants of the same hadith, or the fact that only one narrative path (narrator) of such hadith exists, or the odd status of the transmission chain despite the fact that it has been transmitted through many other paths, this last one being the *gharīb* which is so only *isnādan*, as to its chain, and not matnan and *isnādan* (strange in both its text and its chain).

34. Al-Dimashqī. Hishām b. ʿAmmār transmitted *aḥādīth* from him [Indeed, al-Khawlānī is a few links down in such transmission path]. Most of the comments about his hadith transmission, extending to the accusation of deliberately lying, are highly negative. However, it is particularly the *aḥādīth* which have only been narrated through him that are robustly discarded.

35. *Munkar al-ḥadith* in the text, which is the definition of him given by al-Bukhārī. *Munkar* literally means declared to be unknown. The act of *inkār* is the opposite of the act of *taʿrīf*, declaring something to be known. In short, such a transmitter is explicitly catalogued among those whose narrations are not used as proof.

36. *Al-tawakkul.*

37. *Al-riḍā.* Also satisfaction and pleasure authentically felt in the heart.

38. It has been reported by Muslim in his *Ṣaḥīḥ*, the "Book of *īmān*," and by Aḥmad in his *Musnad*.

39. That is, the Sufi masters.

40. Such passage is omitted from the original manuscript of the Arabic text, which shows a blank.

41. It has been reported by al-Bukhārī in the "Book of *al-Riqāq*" (heart-softening matters) in his *Ṣaḥīḥ*, as well as by al-Tirmidhī in his *Sunan*.

42. It has been reported by Aḥmad in his *Musnad*, by Abū Dāwud, al-Tirmidhī, and Ibn Mājah in their respective *Sunan*, and is widely regarded as a *ṣaḥīḥ* hadith.

43. Five different views have been paraded about to explain the import of such a definition. A modern scholar underpinned the opinion that by it al-Tirmidhī intended the hadith transmitted through a number of narrative chains, some being the chains of the *ḥasan* and others of the *ṣaḥīḥ* hadith, and Allāh knows best.

44. Reported by Aḥmad, Ibn Mājah, al-Ṭabarānī, in *al-Muʿjam al-kabīr*, Abū Nuʿaym in *al-Ḥilyah*, and al-Baghawī in *al-Mishkāt*. It is a good hadith. The word *awjiz* in the text (teach concisely) means to limit himself ﷺ to the essence of the matter to enable an easier grasp of what is taught, or to convey that sought after knowledge by an abridging speech using a few words that nevertheless gather a vast knowledge and a far-reaching meaning. As for *muwaddiʿ* (who is bidding farewell), it denotes the following: Be as if you were praying your last prayer. The signification of *ijmaʿ* (gather) is an injunction that he should firmly believe in, and resolve on (despair vis-à-vis what is in people's hands).

45. In a preceding part of the overall treatise, of which this self-contained unit devoted to *zuhd* represents the third section.

46. Ibn Mājah reported it. In a different and sounder variant it is also found in al-Ḥākim's *Mustadrak*, that is, his *Mustadrak ʿala al-Ṣaḥīḥayn* of al-Bukhārī and Muslim.

47. Abū Nuʿaym quoted it in the biographical account of Wuhayb found in his *Ḥilyah*. The word *qaṣab* in the text signifies any plant with joints (of a knotted stem).

48. Al-Tirmidhī, who described it as hadith *ṣaḥīḥ*, Ibn Mājah, Aḥmad, al-Ḥākim, and Abū Dāwud al-Ṭayālisī (in his *Musnad*) have reported it. The phrase *Mā lī wa li al-dunyā* ("What have I got to do with the *dunyā*!") is the subject of debate. Some say the *mā* is here a letter of negation, i.e., I have no intimacy or love relationship with this World, and this World has no intimacy or love relationship with me, that I should be desirous of it, spread myself towards it, and gather for myself what is in it. Others have interpreted it as a letter of interrogation, that is: What intimacy and love do I have with this World? Or: What have I got that goes along with an inclination towards this World, and what inclination has it got towards me, for I am a seeker after the Next World, and the *dunyā* is its rival?

49. I have not been able to trace this narration to any known source.

50. Refer to the entry of Abū Sulaymān al-Khaṭṭābī in "Appendix Two: Biographical Notations."

51. Meaning al-Fārisī ﵁.

52. His *kunyā*.

53. See the biographical account of Salmān ﵁ in *Ḥilyat al-awliyā'* by Abū Nuʿaym.

54. Ibn Mājah reported it, as well as Abū Nuʿaym in *Ḥilyat al-awliyā'*.

55. Maḥmūd b. Ghaylān al-ʿAdawī (by *walā'*), Abū Aḥmad al-Marwazī (d. 249 AH), the *ḥāfiẓ* who settled in Baghdad. A reliable transmitter who narrated from Wakī', Sufyān b. ʿUyaynah, Abū Usāmah, ʿAbd al-Razzāq and multifarious other narrators.

56. Ibn Abī Sufyān, the great caliph ﵁.

57. His uncle.

58. In the singular in the text, despite the reference to a covenant with "us."

59. It has been reported by Aḥmad, al-Tirmidhī, al-Nasā'ī, Ibn Mājah, and al-

Baghawī in *Mishkāt al-maṣābīḥ*. It is a good narration. The Arabic word in the text, which we rendered as disquieting, comes from the root-meaning of a thick and very stony ground.

60. That is, exercise *zuhd*.

61. An authentic hadith reported by Ibn Mājah, al-Ḥākim, al-Ṭabarānī in *al-Muʿjam al-kabīr*, and al-Baghawī in *Mishkāt al-maṣābīḥ*.

62. It has been reported by Ibn Mājah in his *Sunan* and by Abū Nuʿaym in *Ḥilyat al-awliyā'*.

63. Sūrah al-Baqarah, 2:43 (in the *Warsh riwāyah*, 44 in others).

64. That is, rest in ease, take a metaphorical (or even literal) recumbent position, since his promoting of *zuhd* presupposes that he is not in need of this World and of people's gracious bestowals of worldly lots on him. And provision has already been divinely allotted as the addressee "fully knows."

65. Sūrah al-Ṣaff, 61:2.

66. Sūrah Hūd, 11:88, from the address to his nation by Shuʿayb ﷺ.

67. Sūrah al-Baqarah, 2:272 (in the *Warsh riwāyah*, 273 in others). The word reticence translates the Arabic noun *al-taʿaffuf*.

68. Sūrah al-Maʿārij, 70:5.

69. Sūrah al-Qaṣaṣ, 28:24.

70. That is, in another section thereof.

71. Ibid.

72. That is, asking somebody else for the fulfilment of one's need.

73. The state of asking humans while in need.

74. Meaning such affluent people, who did not stint in granting themselves the benefit of Allāh's gift to them.

75. This narration could not be traced to any known source.

76. In another section of the three-part treatise.

77. See note 10.

78. Al-Tirmidhī reported it, and mentioned that ʿAlī b. Yazīd, found in its chain of narration, is declared weak in his hadith transmission. It has also been reported by Ibn Mājah, Aḥmad, al-Ḥākim in his *Mustadrak*, Ibn al-Mubārak

in his aforementioned work on *zuhd*, and al-Ṭabarānī in al-*Mu'jam al-kabīr*. *Aghbaṭ* (the most fortunate) means the one whose state and final destination are the best. *Khafīf al-ḥādh* (whose social state is slight) is a reference to the person of little wealth, whose back is lightened by the paucity of dependents. The semantic origin of the word *ḥādh* (synonymous with *ḥāl* or state) is that part of a horse's back on which wool is found. As for the phrase *kāna ghāmiḍan fi al-nās*, it signifies the one who, among people, is obscure, concealed, and knowledge of whom is not diffuse.

79. That is, in a preceding section of this work.

80. See note 11.

81. That is, the stony ground known as *ḥarrah al-Madīnah*.

82. It has been reported by al-Bukhārī and Muslim, as it is said in the text. The wording here is Muslim's, found in the "Book of *zakāt*" (chapter on exhortation to give *ṣadaqah*). With variations, al-Bukhārī reported it in three distinct books of his *Ṣaḥīḥ, Kitāb al-zakāt* ("*Bāb mā uddiya zakātuhu fa-laysa bi kanz*"); *Kitāb al-istiqrāḍ* ("*Bāb adā' al-duyūn*"); and *Kitāb al-riqāq* ("*Bāb qawl al-Nabī*" ﷺ "*Mā yasurrunī anna ʿindī mithla Uḥudin dhahaban*"). It is said that the reference to three nights is due to the fact that, ordinarily, one would be unable to dispose of the golden equivalent of such as Uḥud in a shorter time. In this hadith, we detect a strong inducement to appropriately spend aplenty on Allāh's slaves, as well as a majestic indication of his deep concern with the discharge of debts, of his *zuhd* in this world and his encouragement to his ummah to likewise practise *zuhd* in the matter of wealth save for what is stored to satisfy a debt.

83. Reported by al-Tirmidhī who described it, in the transmission form, as hadith *ḥasan ṣaḥīḥ gharīb*, which fundamentally denotes either a hadith transmitted through a number of narrative chains, as in the present instance, some of which display strange elements, or, in other examples, a hadith transmitted through a single chain which al-Tirmidhī was undecided about whether to classify it as *ḥasan* or as *ṣaḥīḥ*, due to the existing divergence of such two opinions on it among the *ʿulamā'*. The meaning is that, once their barley flour was used to make bread, no surplus portion would be left for them, thereby indicating the severity of their material condition.

84. In a starved state. Literally, empty in the stomach (for lack of eating).

85. Reported by Aḥmad, al-Tirmidhī (who classified it in the aforementioned

manner), and Ibn Mājah.

86. It has been reported by al-Tirmidhī, who actually termed it hadith *ḥasan ṣaḥīḥ*, and by Ibn Mājah.

87. The word *ṣaḥīḥ* literally means healthy, sound, wholesome. Its opposite is *saqīm* meaning ill, unhealthy, sick. Al-Tirmidhī's definition of such a hadith concords with that of the *muḥaddithūn* generally.

88. Ibn Mājah reported it, and its transmission chain is good.

89. Reported by al-Bukhārī, Muslim, Aḥmad, and Ibn Mājah.

90. It is reported by Muslim, al-Tirmidhī, who judged it to be *ḥasan ṣaḥīḥ*, and Ibn Mājah.

91. Al-Bukhārī reported the meaning of it (though not its letter), and it has been further reported by Muslim.

92. Cf. al-Bukhārī and al-Nasā'ī.

93. It has been reported by the *Shaykhayn* as in the text, as well as by al-Tirmidhī (in terms of meaning, but not literally), Ibn Mājah and Aḥmad.

94. Cf. al-Bukhārī, Muslim, and Aḥmad

95. Al-Nasāʿī has reported it.

96. Ibn Mājah reported it. We find in its chain of transmission Suwayd b. Saʿīd, concerning whom Ibn Ḥajar al-ʿAsqalānī said in *Taqrīb al-tahdhīb*: "In his own hadith gathering, he was truthful. However, he became blind and started to receive extrinsic hadith." In other words, such reliance on getting and learning hadith he did not personally take down exposed him to the narrations of less than truthful transmitters.

97. Reported with similar wording by al-Bukhārī, as well as by Muslim.

98. This is the same as with the previous hadith in terms of reporting sources.

99. A precise technical term in the lexicon of the hadith-scholars, describing a *muḥaddith* of exalted rank who fulfils a whole catalogue of demanding prerequisites.

100. In its chain of transmission we encounter Sa'īd b. Maysarah, whose credibility has been impugned. Al-Bukhārī ascribed disowned narrations to him, and Ibn Ḥibbān asserted that he related forged *aḥādīth*. In particular, al-Ḥākim linked such forgeries to his hadith transmission from Anas. Yaḥyā al-Qaṭṭān

openly declared him a frequently mendacious narrator. This transmission path is thus regarded as forged, hence our decision to quote it within square brackets. See in this whole regard al-Bukhārī's *al-Tārīkh al-ṣaghīr* and *al-Tārīkh al-kabīr*, al-Dhahabī's *Mīzān al-iʿtidāl* and Ibn Abī Ḥātim's *al-Jarḥ wa al-taʿdīl*.

101. The *ridā'* mentioned in the text is a loose outer garment.

102. I could not trace it to any source. Indeed, the passive form of the verb "it has been reported," without reference to any known collection, has been utilized in the author's text.

103. Cf. Al- Bukhārī, Muslim, and al-Tirmidhī, who described it as *ḥasan ṣaḥīḥ*.

104. See Ibn Mājah's *Sunan*.

105. Such variant.

106. That is, ʿĀ'ishah ﷺ.

107. Al-Tirmidhī, who reported it (Abū Dāwūd, too, reported a similar variant thereof), defined it as hadīth *ḥasan ṣaḥīḥ* in terms of the particular narrative path which he recorded.

108. The wife of the Prophet ﷺ.

109. Cf. Abū Dāwud's *Sunan*, and al-Baghawī's *Mishkāt al-maṣābīḥ*. It is not a particularly strong narration, and weakness has been attributed to it.

110. The two treacherous tribes against which war was waged.

111. Ibn Mājah reported it. The problem with its *isnād* is the presence of Muslim b. Kaysān al-Aʿwar, a weak narrator. Refer to *al-Ḍuʿafā'* by al-ʿUqaylī and the other sources cited in footnote 100 above.

112. That is, dust-colored or earth-colored. It is the diminutive by elision (due to the elision of the first consonant, the *hamzah*, to fit it into the classical morphological form *fuʿayl* of the diminutive) of the word *a'far* bearing the said meaning. See in that regard Ibn al-Athīr's *al-Nihāyah fī gharīb al-ḥadīth wa al-athar*, under the entry "*ʿayn-fā'-rā'*." The hadith is reported in both *Ṣaḥīḥ al-Bukhārī* and *Ṣaḥīḥ Muslim*.

113. Or even: "from the genus of livestock."

114. Al-Tirmidhī reported it, save that the wording handed down by him is different, "*Mā abqayta li-ahlika*?" though the import is identical. He termed it

hadith *ḥasan ṣaḥīḥ*. Al-Ḥākim, too, reported it in *al-Mustadrak* and labelled it *ṣaḥīḥ*, al-Dhahabī concurring with him on that. It is also reported in Abū Nuᶜaym's *Ḥilyat al-awliyā'*.

115. Indeed, it is said by some that Abū Bakr did not love this world, and the *dunyā*, in turn, did not love him, whence inter alia the brevity of his caliphate, by contrast to ᶜUmar who loved it and was loved by it in return, as attested by the length of his rule and the great expansion it witnessed.

116. One wonders how this passage could have been rendered, in a widely circulating English translation of the relevant section of Abū Nuᶜaym's *Ḥilyah*, as "with silk and fineries" [generically], "and they will condemn woollen garments," when no garments are mentioned in the Arabic text, and no need exists, for the readers' sake, to draw a comparison with silk and wool in matters of dress. Had he wished to make such a straight comparison Abū Bakr ﷺ would have done so, but he chose to make a different analogy. In the analogy he chose a special meaning (as well as a species of eloquence) is embedded, apart from the duty of faithfulness to the translated text.

117. The word used in the text is *ḥasā'ik*, the plural of *ḥasīkah*, the gnawed fodder of barley and its like. It is annexed by the genitive construction (*iḍāfah* or annexation) to the word *saᶜdān*, meaning a specific thorny plant (we have generalized the meaning) which is one of the most useful and salubrious varieties of pasture, so much so that a famous proverbial expression elevates it to the paradigm of something preferred over its peers or likes. It also denotes the thorn of the palm-tree. As for *ḥasak*, it is a name of several prickly herbs, especially of the genus Tribulus (*riṭrīṭiyyah* in Arabic). The famous idiomatic phrase of the Arabs is *ḥasak al-saᶜdān*. One says: *Ka'anna janbahu ᶜalā ḥasā'ik al-saᶜdān*, i.e., as if his side were on the ḥasak of the *saᶜdān*, meaning anxiously disquieted, agitated, apprehensively perturbed, as well as restlessly fidgety and disgruntled, and twitching nervously. Abū Bakr ﷺ thus used another figurative expression, tangible and abstract at the same time, referring this time to nourishment instead of attire or bedding. This whole sentence, though, has been ostensibly expunged from the said English translation, otherwise excellent and meritorious in its generality. Granted that some of the words used were not easy or common, but rendering in a foreign language the meaning of the sayings of the sires of the past one seeks to emulate is a trust to be discharged in full earnest, given the present-day Muslims' reliance on such translations thereof.

118. Cf. Abū Nuʿaym's *Ḥilyat al-awliyā'*.

119. Cf. Abū Nuʿaym's *Ḥilyat al-awliyā'*.

120. That is, the job was sloppily done and the fabric started to unravel.

121. So that he could then hem them for him.

122. *Ḥilyat al-awliyā'*.

123. Meaning the grandson of the Prophet ﷺ.

124. *Ḥilyat al-awliyā'*, and Ibn al-Jawzī's *Ṣifat al-ṣafwah*.

125. *Ḥilyat al-awliyā'*. The author of *Muntakhabu kanz al-ʿummāl* quoted it as well, ascribing it to Qatādah from ʿAbd b. Ḥamīd and Ibn Jarīr.

126. To make them more comfortable.

127. Sūrah al-Aḥqāf, 46:19 (in the *Warsh riwāyah*, 20 in others). *Ḥilyat al-awliyā'*. The author of *Muntakhabu kanz al-ʿummāl*, too, quoted it, ascribing it to Abū Mūsā al-Ashʿarī from ʿAbdallāh b. al-Mubārak and Ibn Saʿd.

128. Which are used for seasoning.

129. *Al-qadīd*, jerked meat.

130. *Jaysh al-ʿusrah*, before the Battle of Badr took place.

131. It has been reported by Aḥmad, and by Abū Nuʿaym in *Ḥilyat al-awliyā'*.

132. *Fitnah*, a severe testing of their faith by rifting disunion, et al.

133. Lit., entered.

134. The famous city in Yemen, i.e., an *ʿAdanī* loincloth, one made in such locality.

135. *Ḥilyat al-awliyā'*, where the narrator's name is distorted into Abū al-Malik b. Shaddād. The noun for wrap in the Arabic text is *rayṭah* (also a classical proper noun of women), which denotes a single piece of cloth, not two pieces patched together.

136. Referred to elsewhere as ʿAntarah, the father of Hārūn b. ʿAntarah, who narrated it from Aḥmad b. Jaʿfar.

137. A district of al-Kūfah in this context. The same name was given to the palace of al-Nuʿmān built by the "architect par excellence," the Byzantine Sinimmār.

138. That is, the revenues flowing into the *bayt al-māl.*

139. *Ḥilyat al-awliyā'.*

140. *Ḥilyat al-awliyā'* and *Ṣifat al-ṣafwah.*

141. *Ḥilyat al-awliyā'.*

142. *Ḥilyat al-awliyā'.*

143. It has been reported by al-Tirmidhī, Aḥmad, al-Ḥākim, and Abū Nuʿaym in the *Ḥilyat al-awliyā'*. It is a good narration.

144. Meaning the grandson of the Prophet ﷺ.

145. Reported in *al-Zuhd* by Aḥmad b. Ḥanbal, in *Ḥilyat al-awliyā'*, and in *Ṣifat al-ṣafwah*, where Ibn al-Jawzī ascribed it to Aḥmad.

146. Here the text presents a visible gap between one part of the account and the rest. The full narration as relayed in the *Ḥilyah* from Ṭalḥah's wife Saʿdā b. ʿAwf is as follows: She said: "In one day, Ṭalḥah gave one hundred thousand silver coins as *ṣadaqah.* What held him back from setting out for the mosque was the fact that I tied up for him some money in his robe." The narration is reported in *Ḥilyat al-awliyā'* and *Ṣifat al-ṣafwah.*

147. Not servants or workers as found in an English translation. He thus "owned" such persons [their *riqāb*, not their mere use either], as unequivocally attested by the Arabic phrase *kāna lahu* in the text.

148. That is, he had distributed the same in full.

149. In *al-Zuhd.* It is also in *Ḥilyat al-awliyā'.*

150. Meaning silver coins in all likelihood.

151. His *kunyā.*

152. *Ḥilyat al-awliyā'* and *Ṣifat al-ṣafwah.*

153. Literally meaning the forest or the thicket.

154. *Ḥilyat al-awliyā'.*

155. See Muslim, al-Nasā'ī, and Aḥmad.

156. Al-Shām.

157. Al-Ṭabarānī and Abū Nuʿaym (in *al-Ḥilyah*) have reported it. It is also quoted by Ibn Ḥajar in his biographical work on the companions (*al-Iṣābah*). The narration has a broken chain of transmission.

158. By freeing an equivalent number of slaves in his ownership who headed such family nuclei. Cf. *al-Mustadrak.*

159. The word used in the Qur'ān to describe one of the helpers of Sayyidunā ʿĪsā ﷺ.

160. Cf. *al-Mustadrak.*

161. As an advisory instruction.

162. Al-Ḥākim in his *Mustadrak*, al-Dhahabī commenting on it that Furāt b. al-Sā'ib, found in its narrative chain, was discarded by the reliable hadith transmitters. It has also been quoted by Abū Nuʿaym in *al-Ḥilyah.*

163. Causing himself to be left out as a candidate for the office and thus as a potential choice for the caliphate.

164. The Prophet ﷺ said the losers were those having a huge amount of wealth, except so and so and those who spend their wealth generously on those whom they find in front of them, behind them, on their right side and on their left side, adding that they are a few. How could ʿAbd al-Raḥmān not be one of those few? How could he be one of the losers, *wa ʿiyādhu billāh?*

165. Sūrah al-Ḥadīd, 57:10. Some commentators have referred the allusion to the Treaty of al-Ḥudaybiyyah, though the majority of the *mufassirūn* have taken the word "Victory" to be a reference to the conquest of Makkah. In any case, ʿAbd al-Raḥmān b. ʿAwf participated in both (and many more defining occurrences before).

166. That is, beset by *iḍṭirāb*, a disorderly corruption and disturbance of the equilibrium. It denotes a special kind of deficiency in hadith transmission.

167. See above.

168. Reported by al-Bukhārī, with some minor difference in wording, and by Muslim.

169. It has been reported by al-Bukhārī, Muslim, al-Nasā'ī, Ibn Mājah and Aḥmad (in their respective abovementioned works).

170. It has been reported in the *Ṣaḥīḥayn*, by al-Bukhārī and by Muslim.

171. Reported by al-Tirmidhī. It is an authentic narration. We have rendered the Arabic word in the text *mutakhawwiḍ* as "who hastily disposes of." The semantic origin of the root word *al-khawḍ* is to walk on water and to stir it. It was then employed, figuratively, to signify deceitful obscuring of a matter

and dealing with it (once so stirred and upset by obfuscating commotion). The meaning is thus: How many a person who deals with the wealth of Allāh and His *Rasūl* by what Allāh is not pleased with, i.e., they meddle with the public treasury and dispose arbitrarily of the Muslims' wealth without distributing it. The word *khaḍirah* can be rendered in many different ways, more literal or more figurative. The meaning is that the outward shape of this World is nice and elegantly, pleasantly fine, and the Arabs refer to every shiningly radiant and brilliant thing as a green *nāḍir*. It might be a feminine noun because of the "flower of this World" (*zahrat al-dunyā*) mentioned in the Qur'ānic verse, since wealth encompasses such flower. Or the meaning of wealth in this narration is the dunyā, because wealth is part of this World's adornment. Given that *dunyā* is a feminine word, there would be gender concordance of the feminine *khaḍirah*; the *dunyā* with its adjectival descriptive *ḥulwah* (sweet).

172. Reported by al-Tirmidhī, Aḥmad, and al-Baghawī in *al-Mishkāt*, an authentic hadith. Al-Mundhirī quoted it in *al-Targhīb wa al-tarhīb*. As for the second slave mentioned in the narration, he has the reward of beneficial knowledge on top of the reward for the would-be wealth he would spend correctly.

173. *Al-ghurufāt*, translated hereunder as "high halls of Paradise."

174. Cf. al-Bukhārī, Muslim, Abū Dāwud, al-Tirmidhī (who attached thereto the tag of *ḥasan ṣaḥīḥ*), al-Nasā'ī, Ibn Mājah, and Aḥmad.

175. An authentic hadith reported by Aḥmad and Ibn Mājah.

176. Aḥmad reported it. The *ḥāfiẓ* al-Haythamī quoted it in *Majmaᶜ al-zawā'id*, saying that Aḥmad reported it, as well as al-Ṭabarāni in *al-Muᶜjam al-kabīr* and *al-Muᶜjam al-awsaṭ*, and by Abū Yaᶜlā, the narrators of both Aḥmad and Abū Yaᶜlā being the narrators of hadith *ṣaḥīḥ*. *Al-Ḥāfiẓ* al-ᶜIrāqī stated that Aḥmad, Abū Yaᶜlā and al-Ṭabarāni have reported it from the narration of ᶜAmr b. al-ᶜĀs through a good transmission chain.

177. Cf. al-Bukhārī in the *Ṣaḥīḥ*, Muslim, Aḥmad, al-Tirmidhī, al-Bukhārī in *al-Adab al-mufrad*, al-Ṭabarāni in *al-Muᶜjam al-kabīr*, al-Bayhaqī in *al-Sunan*, Abū Nuᶜaym in *Ḥilyat al-awliyā'*, and al-Baghawī in both *al-Mishkāt* and in *Sharḥ al-sunnah*.

178. Being his *kunyā*, as per footnote 1.

179. That means his independence, whereby his fearless advocacy of the truth

was secured, would be pressurized by persuasive coaxing, which his human state of need would make it difficult to resist or be indifferent to.

180. At this point in the text, the author makes reference to the specific cases of Ṭalḥah, al-Zubayr and ʿAbdallāh b. Masʿūd, who bequeathed wealth in huge measures. The text, as evinced by the printing of the manuscript copy, is quite disjointed and unintelligible at times in these two lines. It further refers to something like the *qantar*, a varying wealth that would bear no meaning for the reader of this translation. In addition, unlike the preceding examples, the species of wealth is not clarified. Thus, even when the sentence "whereas Ibn Masʿūd bequeathed 90,000," which is syntactically conjoined to the immediately preceding phrase, is structurally fine and semantically clear in general, one is left at a loss as to which variety of wealth the unit of 90,000 belongs to, though silver coins would be the likeliest conjecture. The point made by the author is in any event sufficiently conveyed, and the two lines merely tend to illustrate in a graphic form, appreciable in detail by a reader thinking in terms of such weights and monetary estimates, the earning, gathering and bequeathing of wealth (of far from insignificant proportions) by some of the foremost companions.

181. See al-Bukhārī, Aḥmad, al-Nasā'ī, and Ibn Mājah.

182. If he did so, it is not however in his *Ṣaḥīḥ*.

183. Sūrah al-Anfāl, 9:70 (in the *Warsh riwāyah*, 69 in others).

184. Sūrah al-Baqarah, 2:266 (in the *Warsh riwāyah*, 267 in others). One wonders why the said translation was chosen for the second part of the sentence, since Allāh ascribed the verb and thus the action denoted by it to Himself in the Arabic text, saying: and from what We extracted from the earth for you.

185. See Abū Usāma in the Biographical Notations.

186. Ibn Saʿd has reported it (in his *Tabaqāt*), and al-Ḥākim, too, whereas al-Dhahabī has quoted it.

187. Al-Ṣiddīq, meaning Abū Bakr.

188. The word nation translates the Arabic *ummah*, while test renders *fitnah*, which is a punishing trial of one's faith and its like, and literally comes from the expression *fatana al-fiḍḍah*, i.e. he melted the silver. It can also be rendered as straying, perdition, and refractory disobedience. One's *imān*, communal concord, political strength et al. might be "melted away" by the pernicious

effect of *fitnah*. The hadith has been reported by Aḥmad, al-Tirmidhī, who classified it as hadith *ḥasan ṣaḥīḥ gharīb*, explaining his evaluation by adding that it was known to "us" in the version narrated by Muʿāwiyah b. Ṣāliḥ, by al-Ḥākim, and al-Baghawī in *al-Mishkāt*. It is generally regarded as authentic, since the *muḥaddithūn* have endorsed such judgment of its status by al-Ḥākim. The strangeness is thus only in the reported transmission mode used by al-Tirmidhī, though the narration has come down with a *ṣaḥīḥ* chain elsewhere. "Wealth" here means to take delight in it, and fritter it away in amusing diversions, entertaining distractions, and pleasurable pastimes.

189. Sūrah Ṭā Hā, 20:129. It is followed by: the flower of the life of this World [*zahrah al-dunyā*], so that We can test them by it.

190. Cf., as mentioned above, Aḥmad, al-Tirmidhī (who deemed it a hadith *gharīb*, as "we only know it from the narration of Muʿāwiyah b. Ṣāliḥ"), al-Ḥākim, and al-Baghawī in *al-Mishkāt*. It is widely regarded as an authentic hadith, as we have said.

191. Unless the verb in the original text was *kathura*, which is more likely and in greater apparent congruity with the whole speech, in which case the meaning would be: so that the slavehood of the self-exalted and conceited abounded among them.

192. By associating with Him the intermediate causes which He set up as the visible agents of the manifestation of His Lordship over the entire creation. He is *Musabbib al-Asbāb*, the Causer of intermediate causes, but they focused on the latter, being His creation emanating from His creative powers and veiling them from knowing and worshipping the One Causer.

193. The companion.

194. Al-Bukhārī reported it in a slightly different version.

195. Actually, by *ṭūbā*.

196. See footnote 176.

197. Reported by al-Tirmidhī, who said about it: Hadith *ṣaḥīḥ gharīb* in this transmission mode. It is generally considered to be authentic. In the technical vocabulary of al-Tirmidhī, the qualification *ṣaḥīḥ gharīb* is adopted for a narration which is authentic, though strange at the same time, since the *gharīb* encompasses both the *ṣaḥīḥ* and other than it, and the *ṣaḥīḥ* might have been transmitted through various chains or through a single one, in

the latter case combining authenticity with the strangeness or *gharābah* entailed by the presence of an exclusive narration. That is why other than al-Tirmidhī disregarded the "strangeness" of the solitary chain and focused on the authentic status of this particular hadith.

198. Reported by Muslim and Aḥmad. His questioning ﷺ is for the sake of alerting guidance. One derives from the hadith that touching an impure substance such as a cadaver, provided that is not moist on either side, does not engender ritual impurity.

199. Untraceable to any known source. Al-Qurṭubī quoted it with an expression indicating its weakness.

200. A well-known technical term used by the Sufis to describe the seven men by which Allāh protects the corresponding number of the regions of the world. Refer to Appendix One for greater elaboration.

201. Cf. *al-Firdaws*. Al-Suyūṭī quoted it in *al-Jāmiʿ al-ṣaghīr*, attributing it to al-Daylamī and Ibn al-Najjār, based on the narration from Ibn Masʿūd. Al-Sarī b. Ismāʿīl is present in its transmission chain. It is said that his hadith is discarded, Yaḥyā al-Qaṭṭān going as far as imputing habitual mendacity to him. See in his regard the biographical accounts and evaluative statements in (Yaḥyā) Ibn Maʿīn's *Tārīkh*, al-Bukhārī's *al-Tārīkh al-kabīr*, al-ʿUqaylī's *al-Ḍuʿafā'*, Ibn Abī Ḥātim's *al-Jarḥ wa al-taʿdīl*, Ibn ʿAdī's al-Kāmil, al-Dhahabī's *Mīzān al-iʿtidāl*, Ibn Ḥajar's *al-Taqrīb*, and similar standard reference works on critique of narrators. Great *ʿulamā'* of all eras, however, have quoted this hadith.

202. Lit.: If a calamity comes upon you in the circles of variable events.

203. A good narration reported by al-Tirmidhī and Ibn Mājah.

204. An expression which has caused a lot of exegetical difficulties to the students of his work. The best explanation of this ostensibly oxymoronic phrase is that al-Tirmidhī meant by it *al-ḥasan li dhātih* (the *ḥasan* in itself) as defined by the generality of the *muḥaddithūn*, i.e., the hadith with an unbroken chain transmitted by a trustworthy narrator with scant narrative mastery from his qualitative like, reliability-wise, all the way up, being free from estranging exceptionality or defectiveness.

205. Sūrah al-Ḥadīd, 57:19 (in the *Warsh riwāyah*, 20 in others).

206. Sūrah al-ʿUmar, 39:20 (in the *Warsh riwāyah*, 21 in others).

207. Aḥmad and al-Ṭabarānī in *al-Muᶜjam al-kabīr.* Al-Haythamī quoted it in *Majmaᶜ al-zawā'id* and asserted that the narrators of al-Ṭabarānī's report were narrators of authentic hadith save for ᶜAlī b. Zayd b. Jadᶜān, who has nevertheless been shown to be reliable by other hadith experts.

208. Reported by Ibn Ḥibbān, by ᶜAbdallāh b. Aḥmad (b. Ḥanbal) in *Zawā'id al-musnad*, and by al-Ṭabarānī in *al-Muᶜjam al-kabīr.* Al-Haythamī stated about it that ᶜAbdallāh b. Aḥmad and al-Ṭabarānī had narrated it via narrators of hadith *ṣaḥīḥ*. As for the verb *qazzaḥahu* (seasons it), it comes from the noun *al-qazaḥ* meaning spice, condiment, and seasoning. It is what is thrown into the pot like cumin or coriander.

209. Sūrah al-Zukhruf, 43:31 (in the *Warsh riwāyah*, 32 in others).

210. The Arabic manuscript presents a blank space at this juncture. In the absence of that portion of the sentence, the whole meaning of it becomes prey to conjectures and is not easily decipherable. The general thread of the argument is nonetheless discernible: The dual benefit and suitability of what is pure is replaced by a limping, lop-sided, partial, incomplete enjoyment which renders the blanket always too short on one side or the other. The impure-illicit wealth is the target of a stronger counter-claim or the trespassing violation of its true claimant's right.

211. "It" could also be "him," depending on the context.

212. Feeling strong and powerful due to such exalted augustness.

213. Sūrah al-Kahf, 18:44 (in the *Warsh riwāyah*, 45 in others). The preceding part of the verse is: Make a metaphor for them of the life of the *dunyā*. It is like water which We send down from the sky and the plants of the earth combine with it.

214. In the first stage of visible appearance.

215. At this point in the original Arabic text there is an unclear word or phrase, due to the fall of ink on the relevant written portion of the manuscript. However, the context gives ample indication of the kind of expression intended by the author, which the reader can construct for himself.

216. Al-Nasā'ī reported it.

217. One that is undergoing a process of change and transformation.

218. The concealed part of that self's private residence.

219. Cf. *Dīwān* al-Imām al-Shāfiʿī. In spite of the author's comment, it is clear from the verses that it is not the "dogs" which shun it (too), nay, they pounce eagerly on it. The shunning one is the illuminated self that shirks preoccupation with attracting it to its side and grasp. Unless the typing from the manuscript distorted the verb "entice" into "avoid," as dogs are engrossed with enticing this World.

220. Reported by Muslim, al-Tirmidhī, Ibn Mājah, and Aḥmad (in four different sections of his *Musnad*). The *kāfir* has thus the ease and the delights in this World, despite their overall scarcity and their turbidity, intrinsically and comparatively to the unadulterated, abundant and everlasting bliss of the *jannah*. Or one can say: A prison by the side of what Allāh has stored for the *mu'min* in the Afterlife, and a garden by the side of what is prepared for the covering-up unbeliever in it. In truth, both interpretive insights hit the mark.

221. Laid down in the *sharʿīah*.

222. Severe trial.

223. Cf. Aḥmad, and al-Ḥākim in his *Mustadrak*.

224. That is his work devoted to the fourth category of Qur'ānic sciences (based on his own classification), the science of reminder or *al-tadhkīr*. A very important book that has not yet seen the light of publication and exists in manuscript form only.

225. Reported by Aḥmad, al-Tirmidhī, al-Ḥākim, al-Ṭabarānī (in both *al-Muʿjam al-kabīr* and *al-Muʿjam al-ṣaghīr*), Abū Nuʿaym in *al-Ḥilyah* and al-Baghawī in *al-Mishkāt*.

226. Sūrah al-Kahf, 18:45 (in the *Warsh riwāyah*, 46 in others).

227. Sūrah Āl ʿImrān, 3:14. It then says: and heaped-up mounds of gold and silver, and horses with fine markings, and livestock and fertile farmland.

228. It has been reported by Muslim, al-Tirmidhī, Ibn Mājah, and Aḥmad.

229. Reported by al-Bukhārī in its meaning, and by Muslim.

230. Exercises *zuhd* in it.

231. In his *tafsīr* he says: The slave has no way to the disobedience of what Allāh has adorned this World with save by His assistance to him in finding it.

232. By the control of the self directing itself to its appropriation.

233.   It has basically been traced hereabove. A similar narration is found in the "Book of *zakāt*" from *Ṣaḥīḥ* al-Bukhārī, "*Bāb man aʿṭāhullāhu shay'an min ghayri mas'alatin wa lā ishrāfi nafs.*"

234.   In his *tafsīr*, the author adds at this junction: Successful is the one who submits and is provided with sufficient means for a living, and whom Allāh causes him to be contented with such sufficiency. Ibn ʿAṭiyyah (the great *mufassir*) said: My father ⸎ used to say about His statement whose actions are the best [Sūrah al-Kahf, 18:7, see chapter 1]: The best action is to acquire rightly and spend rightly, in conjunction with *imān*, fulfilling the obligations and avoiding the forbidden things in the *dīn*, and doing the meritoriously recommended ones in abundance. Al-Qurṭubī commented: This is a fine statement, concise in its wording and far-reaching in its meaning.

235.   It has been reported by al-Bukhārī, Muslim, Aḥmad (in three different sections of his *Musnad*), and al-Nasā'ī.

236.   The revered companion.

237.   Literally, celibacy.

238.   That is, his *ḥawḍ*.

239.   The chain of transmission (and thus the narration) is *mursal*. The *mursal* hadith is the one in which, at the end of its *isnād*, the narrator after the follower has been dropped. As such, it is a sub-species of the weak (*ḍaʿīf*) hadith. However, there are two types of *mursal*. The *marāsīl* (pl. of *mursal*) ascribed to the eminent follower Saʿīd b. al-Musayyib (as the last link of the narrative chain, bypassing the companion(s)) are the strongest of *marāsīl*. In any event, the meaning of this particular narration is good and its entire contents conform in full with the teachings of Islam.

240.   Sūrah al-Aʿrāf, 7:30 (in the *Warsh riwāyah*, 32 in others).

241.   Sūrah al-Mu'minūn, 23:52 (in the *Warsh riwāyah*, 51 in others).

242.   Sūrah al-Raʿd, 13:39 (in the *Warsh riwāyah*, 38 in others).

243.   In the plural, thus embracing Jābir's family.

244.   In the singular, referring to Jābir alone, since he was the leader of the family by whom the example was set and from whom it was sought.

245.   Sūrah al-Aḥqāf, 46:19 (in the *Warsh riwāyah*, 20 in others).

246.   Usually, of course, the ill-gotten asset has been consumed, and food bought

inter alia with it is simply the by-product thereof, not the prohibited property as such.

247. As part of a tutor's discharging of his duties, inclusive of chastising his pupils.

248. The great follower, too famous, even for his well-known and widely examined interaction with Rābiʿah al-Baṣriyyah to be the focus of succinct biographical details in this context.

249. That is, Saʿīd b. al-Musayyib (the greatest of them all), ʿUrwah b. al-Zubayr, al-Qāsim b. Muḥammad b. Abī Bakr al-Ṣiddīq (the grandson of the first rightly-guided caliph), Khārijah b. Zayd b. Thābit (the son of the lofty companion), ʿUbaydullāh b. ʿAbdallāh b. ʿUtbah b. Masʿūd al-Hudhalī, the mufti of al-Madīnah, and the great Sulaymān b. Yasār, all of them unanimously; as for the seventh, some include Abū Salamah b. ʿAbd al-Raḥmān b. ʿAwf, others list Sālim b. ʿAbdallāh (b. ʿUmar b. al-Khaṭṭāb), and a third group name him as Abū Bakr b. ʿAbd al-Raḥmān al-Makhzūmī.

250. Despite that, since there is no foundational discrepancy between the two stances, ʿAmr b. Dīnār narrated that he had seen none to whom this World had less worth than al-Zuhrī, in whose eyes it had the rank of animal dung, and none for whom the gold coin and the silver coin were more despicably lowly [Cf. Ibn ʿAsākir's *Tārīkh madīna Dimashq*].

251. Allāh says in His Book: *You who have* iman*! do not nullify your* ṣadaqah *by demands for gratitude* [mann] *or insulting words* [adhā] (Sūrah al-Baqarah, 2:263).

252. *Al-Jāmiʿ*, the main mosque of the city where the earliest jumuʿah prayer was held.

253. Reported (in its meaning) by al-Bukhārī, as well as by Muslim, al-Nasā'ī, and Aḥmad.

254. At this point, the following truncated sentence is found: So whoever knows that the specific thing, delineated in its individuality, is not lawful.

255. The signposts. We have already mentioned it when providing a short biographical account of al-Khaṭṭābī.

256. Reported by al-Bukhārī, Muslim, Abū Dāwud, al-Tirmidhī, al-Nasā'ī, Ibn Mājah, and Aḥmad.

257, 258. Some units of *ṣā'*, a cubic measure of varying magnitude. The *ṣā'* in al-

Madīnah, at that time, consisted of four double-handed scoops of some staple foodstuff.

259. We have already ascribed the narration to its textual sources hereabove.

260. Being the *kunyā* of Mālik.

261. Or one could say: Make him comfortable by seating him properly, i.e., in close proximity to my person.

262. The path (or method) of the worshippers.

263. That is, the ruler, who is liable for the consequence of such grant, in his conscience or vis-à-vis a claim by the person rightfully entitled to such property.

264. And thus belongs as of right to the public treasury.

265. *Bayt al-māl.*

266. That is, the unjustly acquired.

267. It is unmixed, though it is a mixture of the aforementioned kind in someone else's hands.

BIBLIOGRAPHY

This is a list of the works referred to or consulted for the translation of the work. Citation of some, from the hadith literature, was not from the very textual sources themselves but from reliable reference works in the field tracing them thereto. Since they are all in the Arabic language, the alphabetical sequence that is followed is that of the Arabic letters:

Aḥmad b. Ḥanbal. *al-Musnad*. Cairo: Dār al-Maᶜārif bi-Miṣr, 1985.

ᶜAsqalānī, Ibn Ḥajar al-. *Fatḥ al-bārī bi sharḥ al-ṣaḥīḥ al-Bukhārī*. Cairo: Dār al-Rayyān li al-Turāth, 1986.

———. *Tahdhīb al-tahdhīb*. Beirut: Dār al-Fikr, 1988.

Baghawī, al-. *Sharḥ al-sunnah*. 2nd edition. Beirut: al-Maktab al-Islāmī, 1983.

Bakrī al-Andalusī, al-. *Muᶜjamu mastuᶜjima min asmā' al-bilādi wa al-mawāḍiᶜ*. Beirut: ᶜĀlam al-Kutub, 1983.

Dāwūdī, al-Ḥāfiẓ Shams al-Dīn al-. *Ṭabaqat al-mufassirīn*. Beirut: Dār al-Kutub al-ᶜIlmiyyah, n.d.

Dhahabī, al-. *Mīzān al-iᶜtidāl*. Beirut: Dār al-Maᶜrifah, n.d.

Ḥimyarī, al-. *al-Rawḍ al-miᶜṭār fī khabari al-aqṭār*. 2nd edition. Beirut: Maktabat al-Lubnān, 1984.

Ibn ʿAbd al-Barr. *al-Īstīʿāb fī maʿrifat al-aṣḥāb.* Cairo: Dār Nahḍah Miṣr.

Ibn al-Athīr, Majd al-Dīn al-Jazarī. *al-Nihāyah fī gharīb al-ḥadīth wa al-athar.* Cairo: Dār al-Kitāb al-Miṣrī / Beirut: Dār al-Kitāb al-Lubnānī, n.d.

Ibn Khallikān. *Wafayāt al-aʿyān.* Beirut: Dār al-Thaqāfah, n.d.

Ibn Manẓūr. *Lisān al-ʿArab.* Cairo: Dār al-Maʿārif, n.d.

Ibn Saʿd. *al-Ṭabaqāt al-kubrā.* Beirut: Dār Ṣādir, 1968.

ʿItr, Nūr al-Dīn. *al-Imām al-Tirmidhī wa al-muwāzanat bayna jāmiʿihi wa bayn al-Ṣaḥīḥayn.* 2nd edition. Beirut: Muʿassasat al-Risālah, 1988.

Jurjānī, ʿAlī b. Muḥammad al-. *al-Taʿrīfāt.* Beirut: Dār al-Kitāb al-ʿArabī, 1985.

Khaṭṭābī, al-. *Maʿālim al-sunan.* 2nd edition. Beirut: al-Maktabat al-ʿIlmiyyah, 1981.

Mālikī, al-Qāḍī Abū Bakr b. al-ʿArabī al-. *Āriḍat al-aḥwadhī li Sharḥ Ṣaḥīḥ al-Tirmidhī.* Beirut: Dār al-Kutub al-ʿIlmiyyah, n.d.

Mubārakfūrī, al-. *Tuḥfat al-aḥwadhī bi Sharḥ Jāmiʿ al-Tirmidhī.* Edited by ʿAbd al-Rahmān Muḥammad ʿUthmān. N.p.: Dār al-Fikr, n.d.

Munāwī, al-. *Fayḍ al-qadīr: Sharḥ al-jāmiʿ al-ṣaghīr.* N.p.: Dār al-Iḥyā' al-Sunnat al-Nabawiyyah, n.d.

Mundhirī, al-. *al-Targhīb wa al-tarhīb min al-ḥadīth al-sharīf.* Beirut: Dār Maktabah al-Ḥayāt, 1987.

Nasā'ī, al-. *Sunan al-Nasā'ī.* Cairo: Dār al-Rayyān li al-Turāth, Cairo, n.d.

Nawāwī, al-. *Ṣaḥīḥ Muslim bi sharḥ al-Nawawī.* Cairo: Dār al-Rayyān li al-Turāth, 1987.

Ṭayālisī al-. *Musnad Abī Dāwud al-Ṭayālisī.* Beirut: Dār al-Kitāb al-Lubnānī / Dār al-Tawfīq, n.d.

Qurṭubī, Muḥammad al-Anṣārī al-. *al-Jāmiʿ li aḥkām al-Qur'ān.* 2nd edition. Cairo: Dār al-Kutub al-Miṣriyyah, n.d.

———. *al-Zuhd.* Ṭanṭā, Egypt: Maktabat al-Ṣaḥābah, 1988.

Shīrāzī al-Shāfiʿī, Abū Isḥāq al-. *Ṭabaqāt al-fuqahāʾ*. Beirut: Dār al-Rāʾidi al-ʿArabī, 1981.

Shinqīṭī, Muḥammad Ḥabībullāh al-. *Zād al-Muslim fī ma al-tafaqa ʿalayhi al-Bukhārī wa Muslim*. Cairo: Muʿassasat al-Ḥalabī wa Shurakāhu, n.d.

Ziriklī, al-. *al-Aʿlām*. 7th edition. Beirut: Dār al-ʿIlm li al-Malāyīn, 1986.

For the translation of Qur'ānic verses, use was made of *The Noble Qur'an—A New Rendering of its Meaning in English*, translated by Abdalhaqq and Aisha Bewley (Norwich, CT: Bookwork, 1999). The reference therein is to the *riwāyah* of Warsh, so the numerical equivalent in the other translated versions is provided whenever any such discordance is present.